HOTEL FIDEL CASTRO

An American's 9 Years in the Cuban Gulag

RICK TOWNSON

La Condesa Press

Florida

Published by La Condesa Press, Florida

Billboard photo on back cover by Tracey Eaton

ISBN: 978-0-9898429-0-7

Also available in e-book editions

Learn more at HotelFidelCastro.net

First edition

ACKNOWLEDGMENTS

This book is dedicated to the men at La Condesa and the Cuban nurses whose kindness allowed me to survive the prison and write about it.

Although this story is my own, this book would not have been possible without the editing and story development skills of Chris Kridler. My greatest thanks to her and Sky Diary Productions.

This book is a completely factual account of my experience from my memory, so any errors in facts are my own. I never got back the notes I had smuggled out of prison, but I reconstructed this memoir based on my recollections, letters, the historical record and the few notes I kept with me.

CHAPTER ONE

Within an hour of our docking in Marina Hemingway, there must have been twenty-five policemen all over the boat. Capt. Know-It-All was trying to convince them that he needed to repair the leak at the propeller shaft so the boat wouldn't sink overnight. They were more concerned with the hundreds of pounds of marijuana stashed on board.

Stunned at our welcome and exhausted from our struggle with a storm at sea, neither of us realized he would never see his boat again, floating or sunk, at the dock here in Havana, Cuba.

After three hours of sitting and watching the Cuban police scurry around, the handcuffs went on, and I was led off the boat to a building a hundred feet away with a half-collapsed roof and a room with no door. By then, my instincts told me to try to protect myself. I started speaking loudly to no one in particular, saying it wasn't my boat and it wasn't my marijuana and I wanted to see someone from the United States embassy. I didn't believe any of the policemen in the room spoke English, and in a few minutes, a young man entered the room and sat down beside me. He started asking me questions in passable English, and I would soon learn that his name was Pedro. Pedro was to be my interrogator for the next thirty-three days.

After two hours or so of his questions and my insistence that I had to get back to the United States for Christmas, which was in three days, officers put me in a vehicle and drove me to what appeared to be a modern-looking jail. A torture chamber wouldn't be in here, would it? After they strip-searched me and took my possessions, they led me up two flights of stairs, where there was a whole new set of jailhouse personnel. All of these young men seem to be about five feet five inches tall, a hundred pounds, wearing green uniforms with small pillbox-style caps. Six of them gathered around me, shouting in Spanish. All I could say was "no comprendo." In my fatigued state, I had the thought that maybe these were all Fidel Castro's sons. I started to laugh out loud. They didn't get my sense of humor. All of them surrounded me and shouted into my face, "Americano, Americano!" They spat on the floor and yelled, "Yo Cubano, yo Cubano, el Cubano! Viva Cuba!"

One of them pulled me toward a closet and issued to me a children's size bed sheet and a children's size mat of felt. Then one of the men took the felt from my hand and put it back in the closet and returned with a different piece, this one stained and foul-smelling.

The officers marched me down a hallway of what appeared to be many storage rooms. They forced me against the wall face-first while I waited for them to open one of the doors. I was pushed into the room but immediately ran into a sharp steel frame and saw the faces of three men. The door closed behind me. There was one small light, and I could see that the sharp steel was the bunk that would be my bed. No mattress. Just steel.

Three other steel beds hung from the walls of this five-by-ten box. On them were one fat man, one skinny man, and one well-built tough-looking guy. With only six inches between the two sets of bunks, I had to turn sideways to shuffle past them to use the bathroom, which was a hole in the floor at the back of the box. One of the guards returned to give me a towel and a cake of a rank-smelling substance that had to be Cuban soap.

The three other men were all wrapped in their sheets because it was cold — about fifty degrees and no heat whatsoever. I lit a cigarette and started smoking while these other guys watched me. How bizarre that a communist totalitarian police state with a jail obviously designed by Stalin would allow smoking, I thought. But

the jailers had allowed me to keep my two packs of cigarettes, as well as my lighter.

I finished one and lit another, trying to think with a
brain that had had no sleep for two days.

"Where are you from?" the skinny man asked me in
English.

I told him Key West, Florida.

"You smoke too much," he said.

"I'll buy more."

"Where will you buy more?"

I just shrugged and waited for the next, inevitable
question: "Why are you here?"

I told him that I was on a sailboat that came into
Marina Hemingway and the police found six hundred
fifty pounds of marijuana on it. But I told him that it
wasn't mine, and that the captain thought they would go
easy on us and let us go. He looked at me and then
looked at the tough guy who was listening to our
conversation.

"No, that's not possible," he said. "You will be in
Cuba for a very long time."

"Bienvenidos al Hotel Fidel Castro!" the tough guy
said in Spanish.

Welcome to the Hotel Fidel Castro!

CHAPTER TWO

When I was younger, I used to laugh at myself and say that anything worth working for isn't worth having. I had always avoided anything that was hard: long-term relationships, marriage, children, a lifelong career.

So when I heard about a boat run from Jamaica to Key West that could net me a hundred thousand dollars, my initial objections eroded all too easily.

Key West was always the place to take it easy. It was a place I came to multiple times as I bounced between businesses.

I worked eight years for Hyatt Hotels as a bell captain in Dallas and New York before my first entrepreneurial stint. It grew out of a vacation a buddy and I planned to take in Germany, where we were going to buy German sport motorcycles and ride them there. The bikes weren't ready in time, so instead, we loaded our own Honda motorcycles on a plane out of Toronto and took a two-month road trip around Europe. I'd never been able to find riding leathers to fit my thin frame nicely, but in Germany, there was a company that made custom-fit leathers at a price so economical, I decided I would buy some not just for myself — I would import them to America. After another trip to Germany to set up the deal, I started my business. I loved it, and I had hundreds of requests for brochures a day. But I had issues. Sometimes I liked partying more than I liked working, and the dollar was falling. As the cost of the suits tripled, I abandoned the enterprise.

I spent time in the Florida Keys, then got into real estate in Naples, Florida. Despite the weak market, I delivered pizzas so I could get by until I got the business going, and soon, I was pulling in decent commissions. I loved real estate, too, but it wasn't enough to keep me satisfied.

I decided to go back to school and spent three years at a community college in Gainesville, trying to finish a year and a half's worth of classes. It didn't work out. I went back to Key West, then on to Fort Lauderdale, where my girlfriend at the time was a chef. The restaurants there had a labor shortage, and I'd met some people in Key West who knew how to get the cheap immigrant labor they needed. I facilitated their hire until I realized the company's paperwork wasn't legitimate, and I bailed again. I went to California with my girlfriend, we broke up, and I came back to Florida, eventually setting up a weight-loss business in multiple locations with a former girlfriend.

Working in the vicinity of North Palm Beach, Florida, I handled all the business aspects of the operation while my partner, Maureen, handled all the front-of-the-clinic aspects. Two years after the startup, I was bored. So I showed my partner how to do my responsibilities, signed over to her all my interest in the business, and left with my girlfriend on my sailboat, bound for Key West. It was the fall of 2000, and this would be my third time living there, after year-and-a-half stints in the mid-1980s and the mid-1990s. On both previous occasions, I got cabin fever, felt the need to be productive and left Key West, only to return, vowing never to leave again.

Living in Key West on the sailboat meant we didn't have to pay the island's high-priced rents. My girlfriend worked as a nurse and I as a taxi driver. Eighty percent of our income was spent entertaining ourselves, and that we did quite well. With more than a hundred boats in the anchorage north of Key West, we were fortunate to have only three other boats anchored within a hundred yards of us. Jerry owned one of them.

Jerry also entertained himself quite well when he was in town. Jerry would leave about every six months and was absent about two months at a time. When he was in town, we would often go out drinking together and invite each other over to dinner. It was at one of these dinners that Jerry finally told us he was a marijuana smuggler. Living in Key West, as I had three different times, I had met smugglers before and listened to their tales of adventure and easy cash. But I had never been interested in that business before, and I wasn't interested now. For me, sufficient cash was OK, and keeping my freedom was paramount. I'd always had the freedom to change my life when I got bored. Playing cops and robbers with federal agents was not my kind of excitement. But my girlfriend liked the sound of it. She complained she had only forty thousand dollars in her retirement account, and she wasn't adding anything to it living in Key West. I told her to forget it.

During a dinner with Jerry in the summer of 2002, he brought up the subject again. He told us he'd made five trips to Jamaica, and now he'd made all the money he needed, with most of it buried around Florida. But he seemed to feel sorry for us, two fun-seeking, life-loving people with no money stashed away.

"I don't smuggle anything harder than marijuana," he said, "and the feds are chasing cocaine smugglers. You'd have to be extremely unlucky to get caught."

"No, no, no," I said, between bites of chicken and swallows of wine.

"You both could make a hundred thousand dollars each for a three-week sailboat trip to Jamaica and back," Jerry said.

Carmen, my girlfriend, went nuts. "A hundred thousand is just what I need for my retirement account!" she said.

"No, no, no," I repeated. "You're a nurse who can make sixty thousand dollars a year, anywhere you want, but never again if you get busted smuggling marijuana."

For two days I listened to Carmen plead. She echoed Jerry: "We'd have to be extremely unlucky to get caught." One night, with enough alcohol in me, I agreed that it would be a great adventure to sail to Jamaica and back.

"It's too risky for you to go," I told Carmen. "I'll go and have Jerry get another man for the trip. If the voyage goes well, you can go next time." I didn't want her to lose her nursing license after going to jail. Misplaced chivalry.

Jerry had someone in mind. His name was Kevin, and Jerry told me the story of meeting him in Havana.

There, American yachtsmen can spend a few months at the dock and partake of the Cuban women who are desperate to earn more than the ten to fifteen dollars a month that Cuban life provides. Kevin fell in love with one of those beautiful young women, Jerry said. She was desperate to leave Cuba, so Kevin sailed back to Florida, raised nine thousand dollars and paid to have her smuggled out of the country. When she arrived in Florida, she spent three days with him, then bolted to Miami, gone for good.

Now, that sure sounded like bad luck to me, but if I had been thinking clearly at the time, I should have recognized the incident as the result of bad instincts and poor judgment. Jerry, a successful smuggler, should have recognized the potential for disaster as well or, allowing superstition, shouldn't have put a man with bad luck on a dope-smuggling boat. But Jerry was being kind, helping both Carmen, who needed more money in her retirement account, and Kevin, who needed to overcome a heartbreak.

No one likes to think of himself as a loser in life. And sharing vast knowledge on many subjects, real or imagined knowledge, can distract people from that fact. So when Kevin proceeded to tell Jerry that Jerry was a known smuggler, Jerry was shocked, to say the least. Years later, we learned the only thing Kevin knew about Jerry smuggling was that Jerry had taken VCRs to Cuba.

After talking us into it, Jerry didn't want to risk himself or his sailboat in a smuggling operation if he was a known smuggler as Kevin had proclaimed. He felt bad, but Kevin felt good and had his own sailboat. Kevin and I could go to Jamaica and back aboard his thirty-five-foot full-keel Chris-Craft, a very capable boat that could handle any rough seas on the voyage. Having only two people aboard would make for shorthanded watches, but we were both relatively young and strong, and I had no fear.

CHAPTER THREE

I n the tiny box at Havana's Villa Marista prison, I asked how long my cellmates had been here. The tough guy said two weeks, the fat man five days, and the skinny English-speaking man, three days. His name was Michael, and he had learned English in school. I asked Michael why he was here. He told me his job was burgling houses, and after many successful years of stealing, he got caught. I asked if he had any type of real job, to which he replied that as a trained bricklayer, he didn't have to go to work, he just went by to pick up his paycheck of eight dollars a month. He made over a hundred dollars a month selling the stolen goods from the houses that he robbed. That was his real job.

The fat man was a hotel bellman. He also made over

a hundred dollars a month and was in this box because he'd been busted obtaining an under-aged prostitute for an American tourist from California. He had a lawyer who promised him that his case wouldn't be a problem because he didn't know the girl was underage.

The tough-looking man was charged with assault for beating another man in a dispute over a woman. The other man was in the hospital in a coma, and if he lived, the tough guy would get sentenced to about two months; if he died, five years.

It was very cold that first night. The weather front that had caused the stormy conditions for us offshore brought high pressure behind it and temperatures in the fifties. I had only a sheet, no blanket, and a thin piece of felt between me and the steel bunk. I have never been so cold in my life. I got very little sleep, because I spent most of my time shivering. The smell of the sewer was overpowering while I thought of how to overcome my catastrophic error in judgment.

The next morning, we were served a breakfast of a stale piece of bread shaped like a hamburger bun and a cup of liquid that they called milk. The jailers pushed it through a hatch in the steel door that was the size of a mail slot. It tasted like sugar water and left residue at the bottom of the cup that looked like ground-up bone. Bone juice. I wondered whose bones they were. I was six-foot-four and a hundred and seventy-five pounds, but I saw I wouldn't weigh that for long. Now I was on the Hotel Fidel Castro diet.

I had not showered in seven days, and when I asked Michael, I was told that water came out of the pipe in the wall twice a day for fifteen minutes. All four of us had to shower within that time, but it wasn't a problem. The air temperature was still cold, and the water was not heated. Three minutes was all I could take.

Two hours later, the steel door of the box opened, and I was yanked out into the hallway and pressed face-first against the wall while they re-closed the door of the box. I was taken downstairs, put in a police car and driven to the docks where we had been arrested. There was Capt. Know-It-All sitting on the boat. The sun was shining, the skies were blue, and there was no wind at all. What a beautiful day it would have been to arrive in Key West, I thought. Also on the boat were Pedro, the policeman who spoke English, and a man with a video camera. Pedro started giving Capt. Know-It-All direction, and it became clear that they were going to videotape a reenactment of yesterday's glorious drug bust. I just sat there, not saying a word, while Capt. Know-It-All proceeded to give his best performance in hopes of pleasing Pedro. He pointed to all the different hiding places of the marijuana almost as if he were a policeman and had just discovered them. After they were finished, I was led to a car to be driven back to my box, but not before I was able to shout to

Pedro once again that I had to be home for Christmas in three days. After all, I was an American, and they should respect our biggest holiday, shouldn't they? Maybe this was a form of denial, too, but that's what I was thinking: Let me go; keep Capt.-Know-It-All.

CHAPTER FOUR

Although I had no fear when I lived in Key West, as we planned our voyage in the autumn of 2002, in time for Jamaica's fall harvest, I felt a sense of foreboding. Alarm bells went off in my head, and my instincts told me, *No, don't go.* My worries started during preparations, as I saw the decisions Kevin, the boat captain, thought were priorities. He bought the material to reseal the propeller shaft as it goes through the boat hull to prevent excessive leaking of water into the boat, but he decided not to install it. Getting only one new battery, and an inferior battery at that, seemed shortsighted to me. His proclamations that room-temperature drinking water was the only beverage needed on a sailboat voyage and not allowing me to bring ice in a cooler on board seemed kooky. More alarm bells went off, but I could drink room-temperature water for three weeks. Not a problem. After Jerry listened to Kevin for a week, his only conclusion was that Kevin was a pseudo-intellectual.

We departed Key West with me waving to Carmen as if I were off on a three-hour tour, though I anticipated a three-week adventure to Jamaica and back. On our second day, we started to cross the Gulf Stream, and I wanted to do a set-and-drift calculation. It would allow us to know the proper sailing magnetic course to arrive at our destination in the Bahamas. Kevin, whom I had already started thinking of as Capt. Know-It-All, declared a calculation unnecessary. He would make mental adjustments on the fly to counteract the current of the Gulf Stream. Capt. Know-It-All's navigational skill took us sixty nautical miles north of our Bahamas destination. When we finally got on the Bahamas bank at North Bimini, he crawled into his bunk and slept for five hours. The man liked to sleep.

We arrived in Nassau, and the weather turned bad and windy out of the southeast, so we were stuck at the dock for four days. Again, I asked Capt. Know-It-All if he would like to repack the stuffing box on the propeller shaft. He said no. The bilge pump ceased to work, so off we went to the marine store to get a new one. He had not investigated why the old one failed, but I concluded it died because it was inexpensive. We had plenty of expense money and could get more if we needed it, so I wanted to get a high-quality, more costly bilge pump.

"No," he said. "The cheapest model will be fine."

"Let's get two of them," I said, "so we'll have a backup."

"No, one will do," said the captain.

We sailed south down the Exumas chain of islands. After anchoring one night, our departure the next morning required exiting a small channel that the cruising guides declared dangerous.

"Let's check on the VHF radio for local knowledge of the tides," I suggested.

"No need," Capt. Know-It-All said, dismissing my concern. "There's deep water on the other side of the channel. The tides won't be a factor."

It was very windy. The whole Bahamas trip should have taken three days, but the weather was always on the nose of our sailboat, forcing us to tack back and forth. Sometimes, we'd wait for the wind to change so the sailing would be better.

That morning, the wind was blowing out of the east, the same direction we needed to sail. We would be using the small motor to get out of the channel, but it wasn't designed to push heavy wind and waves as a powerboat motor was. At eighteen knots, the wind was a formidable obstacle.

Moving from the shallow water into the deep water, against the wind, with the tide coming in, we faced five-foot waves. In the ocean, five-foot seas are nothing. The period between the tops of waves can allow you to ride them smoothly. But with tidal water rushing into the channel, the waves became steep, like five-foot rapids, small mountains to scale over and over again.

We inched along. Capt. Know-It-All hung onto the wheel. I held on at the cabin bulkhead, feeling each jarring impact of the boat on the water as it crested each wave. Were we even going forward, or were we being pushed back? There was no way to go but through. If the bow of the boat were to push slightly one way or another, we could have rolled. With the diesel engine running at full throttle, we were barely able to crawl through the current.

It was the longest three minutes of the trip. When we made it, for an instant, I had nothing but praise for the captain's skills. I was just glad to be alive.

But the alarm bells were going off in my head in earnest, now, along with serious premonitions of doom.

Upon our arrival in Georgetown on Great Exuma, the weather again turned bad, and we had to wait at the dock for better sailing. I telephoned my girlfriend and expressed my reservations about Capt. Know-It-All's ability to complete the trip without disaster. She conveyed my concerns to Jerry, who told Carmen that I was just getting nervous. Everyone gets nervous on their first trip. He said to relax. Everything would be fine. That didn't make me feel any better, so I asked Carmen to fly out to Georgetown and spend two days with me while we waited for good weather. Jerry talked her out of that. So I started drinking rum, and lots of it. It was medicinal, as I tried to drink away the alarm bells in my head.

I was sober the morning of departure, but before we let the lines go, Capt. Know-It-All got my half-bottle of rum out of the ice box and poured it out in the water. "There will be no more drinking on my boat while we're under way," he said. "If you don't like it, you can fly home and leave Georgetown this instant."

I was sorely tempted, but I heard Carmen's voice in my head.

"Listen," she'd reassured me by phone, "if something goes wrong in Jamaica, I have contacts there. We'll get you out of jail. In the States, Jerry and I will bail you out."

But Cuba? None of us were thinking about Cuba.

CHAPTER FIVE

The daily routine in the box went like this: Lights on, an hour of communist news on a radio blared down the hallway, a hockey puck of bread with bone juice through the mail slot, and cold water from the pipe in the wall, which was over the hole in the floor, which was our bathroom. Later came a lunch of rice, watery soup and cassava, known in Cuba as yucca. Dinnertime was more of the same. None of it tasted like anything. Not even a hint of salt or pepper, much less any other spice. The only reason I could call it food was because the other guys said it was. About three hours after more communist news broadcasting in the hallway, our jailers turned off our one small light bulb. By now, I was out of cigarettes and began trading my clothes for them.

After five days in the box, the little men in the green

outfits yanked me out, put my face against the wall and marched me down and around the corner to a row of interrogation rooms. Pedro was in the first room on the right. It was so small that it had the same effect as my cell: relentless claustrophobia. Pedro asked me to write a statement. So I wrote that it wasn't my boat, it wasn't my marijuana, and I didn't know where it came from or to whom it was going. All of that was true, but it was not to Pedro's liking.

Back to the box.

"How long do they keep you here in the box?" I asked Michael, the burglar.

"Until you tell them what they want to hear. They don't care if it takes two weeks or one year."

I couldn't imagine being alive in this box after one month, much less one year. "So if I tell the truth tomorrow, will I get out of here?" I asked.

Michael explained that even if I told the truth tomorrow, I wouldn't get out until I told them what they wanted me to tell them. I had no idea what a communist-police-state-dictatorship version of the truth was.

I felt the life ebbing out of me, but I kept to my story. One week later, I was brought back to interrogation with Pedro. He proceeded to lay out the timetable and every detail of our trip from our departure at Key West until our arrival at the dockside in Cuba. Capt. Know-It-All had told them everything, not sparing me any culpability.

I demanded to speak with the American embassy.

"You don't have an embassy," Pedro said. "You have an Interests Section." He'd informed the Cuban Foreign Ministry of my detention, he said, and that was all he was responsible for. When the Foreign Ministry would contact the United States Interests Section about me, he had no idea. I got no phone call. I could speak to Pedro and no one else.

For this last interrogation session, Pedro had brought with him a young lady who spoke perfect English. I'm sure she could see the pain and anguish on my face and in my body language, and she told me that anything I said could not hurt me. In my mental state, the way I heard her was that a confession on my part would not be used against me. So I confirmed for them everything they already knew from their other source, Capt. Know-It-All.

After I was escorted back to the box by the little men in their green outfits, my fellow prisoners could tell by the look on my face that I had broken down and confessed. Michael told me that he was ready to confess, and the tough guy's victim was out of a coma, so he would be leaving soon to serve two months in prison. The fat man was blaming the California tourist for his extended stay at Hotel Fidel Castro and started bad-mouthing Americans in general and me in particular. I didn't know any Spanish, but I could tell that he was trying to convince Michael not to give me any more cigarettes. It didn't matter, because the next day, Michael ran out.

I had no cigarettes and no visit from an American diplomat, and I was about to lose Michael. After his confession, he said he was leaving for another prison the next day. Though he knew there was a prison exclusively for foreigners, he felt we would meet once more.

"You'll be in Cuba a very long time," he said. "There are many Hotel Fidel Castros."

CHAPTER SIX

No, we weren't thinking about Cuba as we pressed on to Jamaica in the sailboat. The remainder of the voyage south passed uneventfully. Jerry flew in from Florida and, upon arrival, found out that our marijuana had been sent on another boat because we were a week late. We had to wait a week for a new batch to dry.

We passed the time at a small guesthouse in Port Antonio, a cute town at the northeastern coast of Jamaica with about thirteen thousand residents, once a banana boom town and later a popular setting for Hollywood movies. I was happy to be off the boat, while Capt. Know-It-All slept aboard.

I'd convinced myself that if Kevin was going to screw up big, it would be upon arrival in Key West. Jerry told me that he had access to a powerboat, so when we arrived in Key West, we could anchor offshore and unload the weed to the powerboat without Kevin coming into harbor and making a big mistake.

One day, a Jamaican driver took Jerry and I to Negril, on the west end of the island, to see the grower and deliver a vacuum-packing machine Jerry had brought from the States. Afterward, we returned to Port Antonio to await the pickup.

When the appointed time came, Jerry joined us for the hundred-seventy-mile sail west to the rendezvous point outside Negril. We anchored overnight in a harbor along the way. I suggested we get ten gallons of extra diesel fuel at the marina, but Jerry discouraged me. Maybe he didn't want us to be seen, but getting extra fuel was one more precaution we didn't take.

We had to meet the growers at exactly seven on Sunday night at predetermined coordinates a quarter-mile offshore. The dark December evening provided ideal cover for avoiding law enforcement. I was unsure whether officials had been paid off or were simply in church, but there was no one around to interrupt our transaction.

Out of the gloom, three Jamaicans approached our position in an open boat, and the transfer of pot from their vessel to ours began.

I had no idea there was so much dope. It was heavy, too. Bales of plastic-wrapped bricks of pot were stacked all over our deck, and we did our best to stash it out of sight. When the job was done, Jerry left us and boarded the Jamaicans' boat. He would be heading back to shore to fly back to Florida, and we were on our way to Key West.

The boat was full of six hundred fifty pounds of pot, haphazardly hidden. There was no turning back. I banished my fears and gave myself up to fate.

From the western end of Jamaica to the western end of Cuba, the wind was perfect, hitting the sails just slightly behind the perpendicular. In speed and direction, it's what sailors call a broad reach. We set our sails and didn't have to touch them for four days. For all that time, it was beautiful sailing, the kind of weather mariners dream about.

Despite our easy glide northwest toward the Yucatán Channel, I was aware the weather could change. The decision to forgo bringing along extra cans of fuel nagged at me as the wind began to shift.

Capt. Know-It-All was ready to celebrate, thinking we were as good as home, after we rounded Cape San Antonio in western Cuba. But the wind was shifting from out of the southeast to the southwest, and I wanted to listen to a weather forecast to see if a cold front was coming. The reception was so bad that we couldn't hear the weather forecast on the shortwave radio, but I knew the changing winds had to mean a front was coming for us. And that vigorous cold front, I realized later, was interfering with the radio signal.

Jerry had told us that if the weather got bad, we could tuck in behind one of the islands on the northwest coast of Cuba to ride out a storm, and no one would come out to bother us. Twenty-four hours later, when the cold front struck, we had already sailed past any island that might offer us shelter.

It hit us at night. The light raindrops preceded a sudden increase in the wind. The cold front brought with it twenty-five- to thirty-knot winds and fifteen-foot seas. We couldn't use the sails, or otherwise we would be blown to the Cuban coast, so we had to use the motor to keep us away from the rugged shore and the officials almost certainly waiting there.

Oddly, Capt. Know-It-All's boat didn't have a fuel gauge. Instead, he had calculated the fuel consumption of his diesel motor based on one-third throttle. Now, however, we were using three-fourths to full throttle just to stay off the Cuban shore. We had used all of the cans of extra diesel fuel that we had, with no clue as to how long the remaining fuel would last. As the fuel dwindled, I knew we had screwed up. All of our calculations were based on an easy cruise, not this desperate battle to keep away from Cuba's shore. And we'd lost track of how much fuel was left. All I knew was that the two additional cans of diesel that I'd wanted to bring could have changed our fate. At that moment, our fate was anything but certain.

CHAPTER SEVEN

The large and confused waves that were slamming into the back of the vessel were also pushing about five gallons of water an hour into the boat through the worn seal of the propeller shaft, which had not been repacked, because Capt. Know-It-All didn't want to spend thirty minutes to install the new packing material he had purchased just for that reason. We couldn't do it now. It was too late for that. But it wasn't too late for the cheap bilge pump to stop working as well.

We had changed from the usual four hours on the helm to two hours on the helm because it was so strenuous to hang on to the wheel. When I wasn't at the helm, since we had no working bilge pump and no hand pump, I had to get on my knees to scoop the rising water out of the bottom of the boat with a cereal bowl into a five-gallon bucket. The work left each of us approximately one hour every four hours to get something to eat and rest.

Two more days passed in this fashion. There was no way we could sleep, but I tried always to eat something and at least relax through meditation during the one hour I had. Capt. Know-It-All did neither.

When the sun finally came out, the wind had moved around to the northeast, and we had reached a point just west of Havana. It was time to turn north toward Key West. But the wind, still blowing twenty-five knots out of the northeast, would not allow us to turn. It was about noon, and I wanted to tack the boat back and forth until sunset. I expected the wind to die down and shift to the east, allowing us to get to Key West in twenty-four hours. But Capt. Know-It-All had chain-smoked his three cartons of cigarettes since leaving Jamaica and wanted to replenish his supply and get eight hours of sleep at the dock at Marina Hemingway. With six hundred fifty pounds of marijuana on the boat, I thought stopping was crazy. But Kevin insisted that we were going in for the night.

"Don't worry," he kept saying. "I've been here before. They won't search the boat on the way in, only tomorrow when we're leaving, and then they'll just be looking for Cubans. Don't worry."

I thought of throwing the marijuana overboard. I thought of throwing myself overboard. But I was too exhausted even to swim. Too exhausted to conk him on the head and continue on myself. He hadn't eaten or slept in three days, and I'd barely done so. Neither of us was thinking clearly. We sailed into Marina Hemingway on the communist island of Cuba, home of dictator Fidel Castro and the world's most successful authoritarian police state, with six hundred fifty pounds of marijuana on board.

In the years to follow, I had plenty of time to question my decisions and our ever-increasing stockpile of bad luck. Two choices that we made at this moment could only have hastened our capture. For one, when Kevin reported the port from which we sailed to the dockmaster, as was customary, he told them Port Antonio, Jamaica. It was like waving a red flag in front of a bull — we were a vessel traveling a well-known smuggling route, coming from Jamaica, the marijuana capital of the Caribbean. We had taken down our small Jamaican courtesy flag, the traditional pennant broadcasting our destination, and swapped it for a Cuban flag; how could we have made such an obvious admission to the dockmaster? Second, our passports showed stamps coming into Jamaica, but they didn't show we had checked out. Who wants to check with authorities when his boat is stuffed to the gills with pot?

The first thing we saw at Marina Hemingway was a Cuban man with a cocker spaniel on a leash. We were so out of it, it wasn't until thirty minutes later that it dawned on me it was a drug-sniffing dog. First we had to deal with immigration paperwork; second, customs paperwork; and third, the man with the dog.

The dog found the first stash within two minutes. Off ran a customs assistant in a mad dash to retrieve the police. It was a Cuban holiday, and all of the police must have been off on some march to the Plaza de la Revolucion, because it took thirty minutes for them to return with two police officers. I was so exhausted, I didn't even consider getting up and trying to run. It wasn't my boat, it wasn't my marijuana, and I had used gloves when storing the small packages throughout the boat. Capt. Know-It-All hadn't used gloves, and his fingerprints were all over the stuff. I was too exhausted to ask him to say that I had no knowledge of the marijuana or to run for a taxi and the U.S. consulate. Too exhausted even to think. Capt. Know-It-All pointed out to the policemen where all the marijuana was hidden, telling me they would go easy on us if he did.

Oh, really, I thought. "Don't tell them about the bales that we have in the hatch at the back of the boat," I told Kevin. "We'll have something to go home with when they let us go, and it won't be a total loss."

You could say I was detached from reality. More likely, I was detached from the universe. I felt brainless and comatose. Capt. Know-It-All immediately pointed out to the policeman the hundred pounds that were in the back compartment of the boat.

CHAPTER EIGHT

One morning after breakfast at Villa Marista, a young jailer yanked me out of the box, and I was taken down the hallway to a room with a barber chair. There a civilian Cuban stood with a handful of disposable razors, and I was given my first shave in more than a month. At this point, I didn't care if I ever shaved again. I had been reduced to an animal, so why not continue looking like one?

Afterward, taken back to my box, I found on my bunk one of my collared shirts and dress shorts, along with a pair of street shoes from my small suitcase, which I had not seen since I left the boat. Michael said a visitor was coming to see me and that I should change into the more presentable clothes. Sure enough, one hour later, I was taken from the box by two Fidelitos downstairs to the lobby of the building.

Pedro was there, along with two other police investigators and five people in suits and other business attire that I would later find out were Cuban Foreign Ministry personnel. There were also two men that were obviously American diplomats. They introduced themselves and asked how I was.

"I'm a prisoner in a jail obviously designed and run with Joseph Stalin in mind," I said. "Can you get me out of here?"

I found out diplomats never really answer your questions, at least not the important ones.

"What happened?" asked the older American, a serious man who gave the impression of being in the intelligence business.

When I told them I'd confessed, the younger diplomat got out of his chair and took a spin around the room in frustration. "You shouldn't have done that," he said when he sat again. "You shouldn't have confessed. You've thrown away any chance we might have had of getting you out of here."

"There's no way not to confess in this psychological torture chamber," I told him.

I gave them information to contact Carmen, my girlfriend, and let her know that I was here, asked for cigarettes that never came, and asked if they had a diplomatic passport for me, all the while glancing at the front door, wondering if I could make a mad dash for the exit. I didn't have the courage to try to flee, after considering what torture they would have for me when they caught me. With a nod from Pedro, two jailers took me back upstairs to the box.

About four times in the past twenty days, they had taken me to be re-fingerprinted. They were obviously trying to match my prints with the ones on the packages. Capt. Know-It-All had his all over the packages, and I'm sure there were some Jamaican prints as well. One day, Pedro called me out of the box for a trip to the interrogation room.

"Why can't we find any fingerprints on the packages," he said. "Why not?"

"I wore gloves." He got very angry, stormed out of the interrogation room and returned with three very small plastic bags. Pedro instructed me to pluck hairs off my arms and put them in the baggies. I would find out later that even with a hundred percent confessions, they wanted direct evidence that I had been handling the packages. So they manufactured the evidence they needed.

CHAPTER NINE

Thirty-two days after being led into this Hotel Fidel Castro, I was pulled from the box and taken to see Pedro once again.

"Good news," he said. "Tomorrow, you will be taken to La Condesa prison, where you will be more comfortable. And there are other Americans there."

The next morning, I was pulled from the box and taken downstairs, where my personal effects were inventoried. I was handcuffed and put in the back of a police car seemingly made for little people when they stuffed Capt. Know-It-All in with me and we drove off.

"So that's what you call them going easy on us?" I asked.

The policeman in the front passenger seat screamed at me. I don't know what he said, but he probably told me to stop talking. Forty minutes later, we were in a sugarcane field in the middle of nowhere, pulling through a guard gate to meet our new jailers. Welcome to the Hotel Fidel Castro, Countryside Resort.

After about an hour of paperwork, Capt. Know-It-All and I were led to a storeroom and issued our bedding. This time, I got a blanket, and the mattress was a one-inch-thick piece of foam. It looked like a giant sponge that had not yet been cut into pieces. The six-foot-long board that was to become my bed weighed maybe twenty or thirty pounds, but I had so little strength after thirty-three days in the box that I just drug it along the ground.

We were led to a gate of sheet metal through a barbed-wire fence that was obviously the entrance into the prison compound. There were three buildings housing prisoners at La Condesa. The one-story build-ings resembled chicken coops — the old window frames, which once probably held glass, were filled with concrete punctuated with about a dozen round holes that allowed little ventilation. Doors into the building were shielded only with barred gates. Nothing could stop the cold, the rain, the heat and the rats from coming in. Inside were bunk beds for about fifty men, spaced eighteen inches apart. They ran down each side of the building with a walkway in the middle. The floor was cracked so badly that most of this smooth finish had come off, showing the rough concrete underneath. The cracks made the floor so uneven that some of the legs of the bunk beds had to be supported by pieces of wood. Most bunks had twelve-inch fans hanging from the ceiling or attached to the head of the bunk. The fans looked ancient, as if they were from the 1950s, both in design and condition.

The men that were inside greeted us. "The Americans are finally here," more than one of them said. The island boys from Jamaica and the Bahamas were raised speaking English, but I was surprised how many Latin Americans here spoke it as well. Many men were lying in their bunks, and others were in the TV room. There were many upper bunks available, and as I looked around for which one might be the best, a big Jamaican came to me, took my bed board and put it up on top of a bunk next to his. Along came a white man in his mid-twenties, squealing about having someone in the bunk above him. He spoke English like a Valley boy and introduced himself as Dillon. He was from Los Angeles, and his body language suggested that he got a Hollywood name change just in case someone discovered him and his talents. Dillon had been here two months. It dawned on me, this must be the American busted with the underage prostitute the fat man from my thirty-three days in the box told me about.

"Screw you, Dillon," said the big Jamaican, whose name was Howie. "Be nice to your fellow American." He put Capt. Know-It-All and his bunk board right next to me. Great.

The inmates knew of our impending arrival, because the Bahamians that were in the prison had family members bring them newspapers. They had read the story of two American sailors lost at sea in a one-month-old newspaper, and then about the arrest in Cuba of two American marijuana smugglers in a three-week-old newspaper. Welcome to the Hotel Fidel Castro.

CHAPTER TEN

Howie told us what we needed to know while he showed us around the rest of the building. At the front was a television viewing room showing Cuban programming on a TV hung from the ceiling, with concrete benches for seating. There were also numerous plastic chairs that, Howie explained, the prison officials allowed the men to purchase. Some of the plastic chairs were so old that they had broken and been repaired with screws, wire and wood. Frankenstein chairs. None of the men in the room were watching the TV; they were playing backgammon or cards. Most of them said hello, but their faces said welcome to hell.

At the other end of the building, there was a small room with men cooking on hot plates. Some of these hot plates were of the Cuban variety, made out of car brake drums. Howie explained that because the food was so bad, the foreign embassies pressured the Cubans to allow the prisoners to cook for themselves. I knew the food was bad, but what they were cooking didn't look much better. The vegetables they were using looked way too old to be edible. And the flies — hundreds of flies. "As soon as winter is over," Howie said, "there will not be hundreds of flies. There will be a thousand flies."

Behind the small kitchen were the bathrooms and showers. There were three concrete troughs, with water pipes feeding each one. One was for brushing your teeth and shaving, the next was for washing your clothes and sheets, and the third was for washing dishes, pots and pans. All of the faucets were leaking, and most of them had string tying them closed. The concrete troughs appeared to have fifty years of petrified scum on them.

Behind the troughs were four holes in the floor: the toilets, with years of petrified excrement on them. Howie told us we were to throw a bucket of water in the hole first to wash the rats away so they didn't come up and bite your balls. After we were finished taking a dump, we would have to toss in another bucket of water.

"Are they ever cleaned?" I asked.

"Yes," Howie said, "every day, with water and a brush." No soap. Once a month, the prisoners got a bottle of diesel fuel for cleaning the toilets, and the smell of diesel clashed with the ever-present smell of the sewer. And here, there were more flies. Hundreds more flies.

On the other side of the wall from the toilets were the showers. Six pipes stuck out from the wall with no showerheads on them. Each had only one faucet handle, because, of course, there was no hot water, so no hot water handle was needed. I checked the water temperature, and it was very cold. It was well water, so it was relatively clean in appearance, but this was January, and even in Cuba, it felt ice cold. There were four walls to the shower room but only bars for a ceiling. When it was forty-eight degrees outside, it was forty-eight degrees in the shower room as well. As a matter of fact, there were so many of these chicken-coop-looking window frames in the building that during the winter, the temperature on the inside was the same temperature on the outside. The only source of heat was the stoves used for cooking.

This building was unfit for human habitation. In any civilized country, it would have been condemned a long time ago. It was a nice place if you were a rat or a fly. I didn't care. I was out of the box and alive. This indignation before me now seemed okay. For now.

I went and retrieved my prison-issue towel and soap so I could take my first shower in Cuba without worrying about stepping in a toilet hole in the floor. Someone offered me a bar of soap that had a wrapper on it and actually smelled like soap. I gladly accepted and went off to the shower room. It was late afternoon and reasonably warm with no wind blowing, so the shower was no more torturous than the ones I had taken in the box in downtown Havana.

Shortly after my shower, I heard a bell toll three times. We were allowed to wear our own clothes, and I dressed quickly. Cotton instead of prison polyester. I was told by one of the men this was the signal to prepare for dinner. Each day, the three buildings would rotate who would eat first, second or third. We were in building three, and today, building three would eat last. Many of the men were very hungry and would line up quickly after the sound of the bell. A quarter of the men never ate the prison food. They either cooked for themselves or had hired someone to do the cooking for them. When it came our turn, one of the guards opened the door and announced that everyone had to line up. We walked single file to the prison dining room between buildings one and two. It took about ten minutes to get to the beginning of the serving line, where I could see that it was the same crap they served to me for thirty-three days in the box. I felt starved for nutrition. I ate it.

Back in building three, Dillon, the other American, explained to me that not only is the food of no nutritional value; there is not soap to wash the prison dishes, pots, or pans properly. The kitchen was outside the prison fence, and though it didn't have soap, either, it had hundreds of flies of its own. I soon realized a pig farm right behind the prison was the source of the flies and the awful, overbearing smell of pig shit. Pete, a Bahamian, had been here six years and had never eaten the food served by the prison. That night, Pete shared with me what he had cooked for the day. I got a big bowl of pasta with some canned meat and spaghetti sauce. It tasted great. Pete asked what a white-skinned, blue-eyed, seemingly intelligent American was doing here, so I told him, reliving the painful decisions and bad luck that had brought me here.

It wasn't easy telling my family the story, either. "I am so sorry," I wrote my mother in January 2003. "I've let you down before, but this tops them all, doesn't it?"

CHAPTER ELEVEN

I learned that the embassies brought their citizens food. Some prisoners had Cuban girlfriends and wives who brought food, and they did a little business selling some to the other men. Carmen was coming to Cuba in three weeks, so I began to prepare a list for her.

On the U.S. Interests Section consulates' first visit after our arrival at La Condesa, they brought old magazines, vitamins, writing paper and envelopes, and one protein bar. This would be the normal care package of every consulate visit in the future. They also brought three emails for me: one from my ex-business partner, one from my eldest brother and one from my sister. When I returned to building three with my small box, five or six prisoners gathered 'round to view the contents of the box while I read the emails.

Maureen was not just an ex-business partner; she had been at first my girlfriend, then my best friend, for eleven years. She wrote me she would do anything to help me get out of here. Her letter moved me to tears, but I would write her back and tell her there was nothing she could do. I didn't want to drag the greatest person I had known in my life through years of futility.

Carmen wrote loving emails that were passed through the U.S. Interests Section to me, but despite her warm words, I could hear her frustration. "My world is so empty without you in it," said one of her letters. "I'm trying so hard to be strong and positive, but some days the pain is unbearable."

I was reading the emails from my brother and sister when one of the guys asked what they said. My brother and sister were of a very common American mindset of personal responsibility. The emails offered appropriate words from my siblings.

"My brother says, 'Just remember, what doesn't kill you, only makes you stronger,'" I told them. "My sister writes that I should take it like a man."

The other prisoners looked at me with disbelief. All the Latin Americans and island boys that had been caught smuggling were of a very close family structure. They didn't smuggle dope to live like a rich man; they did it because they could not feed and house their families otherwise. Their families' sympathy and shared sorrow were with them every day of their prison sentence. They couldn't understand how anyone could be told to suffer the Hotel Fidel Castro and take it like a man. But from then on, in the years to come, when my face would show the pain of the constant dehumanization, someone would say to me, "Take it like a man!" in the tone of gallows humor. When other men's family would visit through the years, I would be introduced as the American whose sister said, "Take it like a man!"

CHAPTER TWELVE

Dillon, two Puerto Ricans with American passports, two Filipinos, and two or three Europeans were the only gringos at La Condesa. All the other hundred and ten prisoners were either from the Caribbean islands or from Latin America. Building one had eighty-four bunks with sixty men; building two had thirty-six bunks with thirty-six men; and building three had forty-seven bunks with twenty-four men. That would change in the months to come, but for the time being, the three chicken coops labeled buildings one, two and three were not overcrowded with men — just overcrowded with flies, the smell of sewer, and the stench of pig farm.

Carmen came and brought me three suitcases full of stuff. The prison provided nothing for the men beyond the bedding, so my list had included everything I could think of, from toothbrush and toothpaste to clothes to food and pots and dishes and plastic utensils. When my mother heard of my list, she asked Carmen whether I was setting up house. In a way, I was. I had no idea how long I would be here. Carmen said she and my mother were in contact with people to try to get me released. She was here for a week, and we had visits every day, including three conjugal visits. I almost felt human again until the day came that I had to say goodbye and watch her leave.

"Enjoy it while it lasts," Pete told me. "Girlfriends rarely stick around longer than two years."

"Well, I'm not going to be here two years," I said.

Pete just laughed.

CHAPTER THIRTEEN

Pete was a Bahamian who had been in the smuggling business a number of years. He had been prosperous enough that he didn't make the boat trips to Jamaica and back. He hired other men to do so. But he had been bored and feeling adventurous, so he'd decided to go on a run to Jamaica.

His speedboat left Jamaica after dark and had engine trouble five miles off the coast of Cuba. The engines would operate only at idle speed, so the crew of five made the decision to dump the dope overboard, clean up the boat to remove any possible evidence, and idle into Cuba with the agreed-upon story that they were just recreational boaters on their way to the Bahamas.

The next morning, while they were walking on the beach trying to find a place with a telephone, they were picked up by the police and taken to jail. They had no phone calls and no consulate visits. But after three days of questioning with everyone sticking to the story, officials took Pete, as the captain, to a section of beach far from where their boat landed. There, the police pointed to a bag in the brush and told Pete to pick it up. Pete, who had never seen that bag, refused, so a policeman picked it up, took Pete back to jail and started writing his report describing the bag on that beach, and many others that they would find, as belonging to Pete and his crew. In all those bags was marijuana, and Pete was charged with marijuana smuggling and given a fifteen-year sentence, as was his crew. The case was fabricated, because Pete wasn't hauling marijuana from Jamaica to Cuba. The dope he and his crew had thrown overboard five miles offshore was cocaine.

CHAPTER FOURTEEN

About two weeks later, two new American prisoners showed up. Douglas Moore was an American living in the Bahamas, and Paolo was a Brazilian-American. Douglas had severe scars on one of his legs, where he had been attacked by a shark during a spearfishing expedition. Howie, the big Jamaican, considered himself the boss of our building and the official nickname-giver. He called Douglas "Sharkey." Sharkey was a very funny man with a big imagination, which he drew upon to tell many stories that were obviously untrue. Sharkey was tenacious, and it was very important for him to make people believe his tales. He would spend hours trying to convince someone of something absurd. He also liked to taunt the guards and officials. If he wasn't being disobedient, he wasn't happy.

Now there were five Americans in La Condesa. But Paolo was pretty smart. He and his family, along with the Brazilian embassy, fought to have him listed as a Brazilian. Everyone knew that Americans were the enemy of Fidel Castro, and that was not a label he wanted. Paolo started seeing the Brazilian consuls when they came once a month, so no one considered him an American any longer.

About that time, a new American showed up. Howie called him Doc. He was a psychiatrist in New York City with a medical degree from Mexico. Paolo out, Doc in. Five Americans.

This was the spring of 2003, and the other prisoners had never seen any Americans at La Condesa. All five of us were facing long-term prison sentences, but no one expected the Cubans to hold us for very long. The general thinking was that they were afraid to provoke the American government or American public opinion. I had heard stories while living in Key West in the 1980s and '90s about Americans getting arrested in Cuba and sent home within weeks. Whether it was during fishing tournaments or sailing regattas, no matter the type of crime, all were sent home. Of course, all Americans knew that Cuba was a police state, so no one would be stupid enough to commit a serious crime. I had always considered myself as a man of average intelligence. Guess I was fooling myself.

I was told by one of the American consuls that there

were two hundred Cuban-Americans in prison, but they were kept with the other Cuban prisoners and not allowed to receive visits from the consulate. Fidel Castro arrested anyone he wanted for any reason, and most of these Cuban-Americans had escaped Cuba, become American citizens and returned at their own peril. There was one exception. Juan was kept with the other Cuban-American prisoners, but he was allowed to receive a visit from the consulate every three months, like us five gringo Americans. Juan was born in America of Cuban parents, and he was a baseball scout by profession. One year before he came to Cuba, he told me, he was in the Dominican Republic watching a baseball game between the Dominicans and the Cuban national team. He managed to get his business card in the hands of one of the Cuban baseball players but didn't speak to him or any other player, and the player never contacted him. One year later, he had come to Cuba to visit his relatives with no intention of conducting any baseball scout activities. He was arrested and given a fifteen-year sentence. He had committed no crime in Cuba but made the mistake of trying to recruit Fidel Castro's property. Juan would spend thirteen years of his life rotting in the Hotel Fidel Castro, Big House.

Every week, more gringos arrived — from Canada, from Italy, from Switzerland, from India, from Germany and other countries — all white guys, and most under bogus charges. At about the same time, Fidel was arresting Cuban dissidents and democracy advocates. Seventy-five Cubans went to prison that spring for voicing their opinion about wanting to live as free men. Democracies from around the world were condemning Fidel and making plans to cut off their economic aid to Cuba. When a country would denounce Cuba's actions, within weeks, one or more of their citizens would show up as a new prisoner at La Condesa. All the charges were either trumped up from petty offenses or outright manufactured. It seemed that Fidel wanted to give the Western countries their own citizens to worry about instead of his citizens, who were none of their business. But the Western countries would not take Fidel's bait. They never complained publicly or in the press about Cuba arresting their citizens. They told their citizen prisoners that there was nothing that they could do. We should not have come to Cuba.

There were at least fifty of us gringo prisoners now here at La Condesa. I wondered if Fidel was trying to get to seventy-five gringos to match his seventy-five dissidents. All of our families were doing everything they could to try to obtain our release, to no avail. Most of the world was focused on George W. Bush's invasion of Iraq, and it appeared that Fidel Castro ingeniously used the distraction to near-perfect conclusion.

CHAPTER FIFTEEN

The Netherlands Embassy would bring their citizens old newspapers. The representatives came once a month and would bring *International Herald Tribune* newspapers that were up to four months old. After reading a few of them, I found the man who was getting the newspapers. As in any prison, everything here had value, and he was getting no money from the outside. He was happy to provide me with the first reading of the old newspapers for thirteen dollars a month. He told me he also got magazines. Would I be interested in any of those, such as *The Economist*? "Sold!" I said. *Time*? "Sold!" *Newsweek*? "Sold!"

Soon I was spending almost thirty dollars a month on reading material. I was a news junkie, so to me, it was money well spent. I read every word on every page, and it didn't matter if they were four or five months old. The only problem was that the prison censors tore out all the news articles about Cuba.

The man who was the previous custodian of the newspapers was also a news junkie. His name was Amadoo, and he was a three-hundred-pound African who would tune in the BBC on his shortwave radio every day — that is, when he was not playing tennis. A three-hundred-pound Nigerian racing around a rock-strewn tennis court as if he were Andre Agassi was one of the funniest visuals I had ever witnessed. We would listen to the almost daily reports of Cuba arresting more dissidents and the international reaction to it. As the days passed, it became more obvious that we were screwed. We all felt like hostages as we realized our countries had no intention of playing Fidel's game.

I would have gone to prison in any country in the world after being caught with six hundred fifty pounds of marijuana, but I still felt like a hostage. These other men who had trumped-up charges still couldn't get help from their countries' governments. It was hopeless.

CHAPTER SIXTEEN

It may have been hopeless, but Paolo had a plan.

Paolo, Sharkey and I often played cards in building three, and Paolo and I had become close. A Brazilian-born U.S. citizen, he was the American I got along with the best. While the others mocked me for getting on a boat with a captain who made such poor decisions, Paolo felt sympathy for me.

The Cubans now looked upon Paolo as a Brazilian, not a hated American. His prestigious family in Brazil had high connections and had lobbied for his release, so far unsuccessfully, but he had another kind of connection — a Cuban-American Miami mobster who'd thrown him a job or two.

"I have a plan," Paolo told me. "My family is still working to get me freed through diplomatic channels, but I may have another way out."

"What do you mean?'

"Remember, I told you I have a construction business? I originally bought a couple of these Caterpillar backhoes from this guy, and he hinted I was getting a good price because they'd been stolen from California. I got to know him and did a few jobs for him, hijacking tractor-trailers coming out of Port Everglades. He has connections in Cuba, and he can get me out," he said. "Do you want to come along?"

Did I want to come along? I'd had a lot of time to think, and I'd worked out a plan for what I'd do when I got back. I had already worked in the weight-loss business, and I thought an online diet store would do well. But I'd have to get back to the States first.

"What would I need to do?"

"Come up with fifty thousand dollars," Paolo said. His brother had made arrangements with the Miami connection to stage Paolo's escape. The mobster had contacts in Cuba who could pay off police officers from Havana to obtain the proper paperwork, drive to La Condesa and check Paolo out of the prison for further questioning at the downtown Hotel Fidel Castro. Paolo — and I — would be allowed to escape from the police car.

Was I interested? Of course I was. Between Carmen, her family and my family, I felt confident I could raise the money, though I hated to ask my family for it. I'd already refused visits from my mother, sister and eldest brother, because I didn't want them to see me in these horrible conditions. Paolo explained that his mother was working with contacts in the Brazilian government to get him released through normal channels. The plan with his brother and the Cuban mobster in Miami would be on hold until it was needed. If Paolo didn't need it, it would still be there for me.

From that point forward, my hopelessness eased somewhat. If worst came to worst, I had at least a way to attempt to get out of here.

Even though I felt better, the general mood of the prisoners was bleak. Fidel Castro had come on the television and made a speech about Cuba cracking down on dope smugglers. I think part of it was in response to George W. Bush's speech that spring criticizing Cuba. But it sure seemed convenient that now, as Fidel had all these gringo prisoners, he also took the opportunity to almost double the prison sentences. Just like that, with one speech on television, prison sentences went from fifteen years to thirty years. It didn't matter if it was one ounce or five hundred pounds; marijuana, cocaine or heroin all got the same sentence, with no mitigating circumstances whatsoever. I had not even been charged yet, much less knew of a possible sentence, but now thirty years was looking like my number.

CHAPTER SEVENTEEN

Cuba has been effective at keeping drug trafficking down partly because demand for drugs in the impoverished country is low. Most Cubans can't afford pot; a marijuana cigarette there costs about five dollars, according to the Just The Facts website. That's a week's pay for a state employee. Harsh sentences for drug traffickers, of which I was all too aware, also have played a role in keeping drug use down in Cuba.

Cuba takes drug enforcement seriously. According to the Foreign Policy Research Institute, in the decade starting in 1988, Cuba increased sentences for dealing drugs; activity that used to earn seven to fifteen years in prison now would get twenty years to death. The United States and Cuba sometimes exchanged information to aid in drug enforcement. Given their cooperation, it's possible I wasn't the U.S. diplomats' favorite citizen prisoner.

"Since the September 2000 addition of a U.S. Coast Guard Drug Interdiction Specialist (DIS) to the U.S. Interests Section in Havana," said a State Department report concerning smuggling in 2002, the year of my arrest, "Cuban authorities occasionally have provided that officer information and assistance on specific cases and he has been able to reciprocate on a limited number of cases." But the Cuban government, the report said, was not "forthcoming on the extent of narcotics transiting Cuban soil and the level of rising domestic drug consumption." In addition, the U.S. official was continually harassed by Cuba's State Security agents, who intruded on his home and vehicle and kept him under surveillance.

"Cuban officials have pointed to the growing quantity of drugs seized over the past few years as a sign that Cuba's attractiveness as a transit point is increasing and interdiction efforts are improving," said the International Narcotics Control Strategy Report, issued in March 2003. While Cuba only selectively released data on its drug-fighting successes, it said the Border Guard at Marina Hemingway detected drugs on at least three U.S.-flagged vessels in 2002. It's unclear if ours was among them. Two of the reported smuggling boats were ordered out of the country. We weren't so lucky.

At this time, according to a United Nations report, a

hundred sixty metric tons of marijuana were coming out of the Caribbean yearly, with eighty percent of it going to the United States — still a lot less than the islands exported in the 1980s.

But you don't have to smuggle drugs to get arrested in Cuba. It's a lot easier than that, and Americans with a romantic notion of the beautiful tropical nation may be in for a reality check.

The State Department warns Americans who want to travel there: "In recent years, the Cuban government has detained U.S. citizens it suspects of engaging in activities perceived to undermine state security. In 2011, it sentenced one such U.S. citizen to a lengthy prison sentence on arbitrary charges after a two-day show trial. U.S. citizens traveling to Cuba should be aware that the Cuban Government may detain anyone at anytime for any purpose and should not expect that Cuba's state security or judicial systems will carry out their responsibilities according to international norms."

This warning alludes to the arrest of Alan Gross, a subcontractor for the U.S. Agency for International Development. He was arrested in December 2009 and sentenced to fifteen years for bringing illegal communications gear into the country — gear that would allow religious and other groups access to satellite Internet; in other words, information not controlled by Cuban censors. Cuba said Gross committed "acts against the independence and territorial integrity of the State." By his own account in spring 2013, the American had lost more than a hundred pounds in Cuban jail. Despite high-level pleas and demands for his release, at this writing, near the end of 2013, he was still imprisoned.

The U.S. Interests Section has this to say about being arrested in Cuba:

"If you or any U.S. citizen is arrested in Cuba, ask the authorities to notify a consular officer at the U.S. Interests Section immediately. The American Citizen Services Unit is not routinely notified of the arrest of dual Cuban-American citizens so it is important that the family notify the Interests Section immediately in these cases. The Interests Section cannot negotiate or secure a U.S. citizen's release from jail (as U.S. citizens in Cuba are subject to the laws of Cuba), but the American Citizen Services Unit can help protect your legitimate interests and ensure that you are not discriminated against. The American Citizen Services Unit can also provide a list of local attorneys, visit U.S. citizens in jail, and contact family members on the U.S. citizen's behalf. We can also transfer money, food and clothing to prison authorities from relatives."

In other words, the American diplomats might be able to make our stay marginally less hellish, but they wouldn't be able to get us out, and normally, they wouldn't even be notified we were there.

CHAPTER EIGHTEEN

One of the new gringos in La Condesa was a wealthy Italian of about sixty-five years old. His name was Franco. He had a home here with a Cuban wife and liked to go bar hopping with the Italian ambassador's son. On one such excursion, Franco was driving his car, with the ambassador's son and his Cuban date in the back seat. The ambassador's son had given money to the Cuban girl so she could score some coke for herself, which she did. She snorted it, and then she died. The ambassador's son immediately bolted back to Italy. After a thorough Cuban investigation, it was found that the Cuban coke dealer had noticed that the white powdery substance inside fluorescent light bulbs resembled high-quality cocaine. It was also full of mercury. He had used it to cut the cocaine to enlarge his profit margin but went to prison for homicide instead. But one criminal is not enough in Cuba, especially when you have a rich old Italian who could be blamed for driving the car. It didn't matter that he had no knowledge that she had purchased cocaine and snorted it in his back seat. Don Franco, welcome to the Hotel Fidel Castro, Countryside Resort!

Until now, there were two prisoner-owned refrigerators at La Condesa. Both of them were in building two. Don Franco was allowed the first refrigerator for building three and utilized it to the fullest. It was stuffed full of food, which was replenished every week. Don Franco hired himself a cook and proper serving staff, by which I mean a gay guy from Columbia. His name was Alex, and Alex also did Don Franco's laundry for him and made his bed each day. Soon Franco was living like, well, an Italian don.

It was amusing for all the prisoners in La Condesa to watch Alex pampering Don Franco from sunup to sundown. Everyone was kind to Alex, even the homophobic island boys. It was like having a girl in the prison block — not my kind of girl, but a girl nonetheless. Soon Don Franco was having small dinner parties inside building three. Some people had plastic card tables, and they would push two of these between rows of bunks and add two plastic chairs, making seating for six.

CHAPTER NINETEEN

Carmen came again at the end of June and brought me two large suitcases full of stuff. She also brought five thousand dollars from my mother to hire a Cuban lawyer. I had already been told that Cuban lawyers were a waste of money. In the past it was possible to buy your way out of Cuban prison, but Fidel had ended that opportunity three years ago. Now, with me facing smuggling charges as an American while Fidel Castro collected hostages of all nationalities, paying five thousand dollars for a Cuban lawyer would get the same result as just burning the money. So during Carmen's first day visiting me, I told her to go and buy me a brand-new refrigerator, have it delivered to the prison and not to take no for an answer from the prison officials. By the end of June, it had become so hot inside building three that the temperature topped one hundred ten degrees every day. She showed up with the refrigerator two days later and spent three hours telling the officials that she was a nurse and that I suffered from heat exhaustion even before coming to Cuba. It was medically dangerous for me not to have ice and cold water, and did they want an American to die in their prison? They relented, and I had the fourth refrigerator in La Condesa, which I shared with all the men in building three. Cold water for everyone!

In answer to my sister's concerns about my health, I told her I was eating better thanks in part to the protein-rich food Carmen delivered.

"My mental health is what's at stake here," I wrote.

The complete control of information in Cuba was absurd but had been effective for fifty years. Now that the world had the Internet, the government needed to show the people that they were as advanced as any country. They couldn't give the people Internet access, but they could demonstrate how the government used the Internet to obtain information and distribute it via the nightly news broadcast.

Not only did Fidel Castro not let information come into his slave country; it couldn't go out, either. All foreign prisoners being released had every scrap of paper with writing on it taken from them by state security before boarding a plane. It didn't matter if they had an address book or any other personal paper when arrested; it was all taken away. And, of course, no one in their right mind wanted to stay and argue with Cuban state security. So I started sending out with Carmen my notes and other important information for safekeeping. My incredulity at what I was experiencing compelled me to write down what I witnessed.

CHAPTER TWENTY

A Canadian had arrived a month before. Perry had been at another prison for the last three months, Combinado del Este, Cuba's show-case prison — or at least they thought it was. I nick-named it The Big House. Built in the 1970s, it had three cell blocks, each the size of a football field, and all were four floors tall. It held ten thousand prisoners all living like rats. I had been there two months previously for a three-day visit to its prison hospital. I went to allow a specialist to look at my knee problem, but after arriving and seeing the deplorable conditions, I started asking for my immediate return to La Condesa. The hospital was run-down and filthy, and with the tuberculosis ward adjacent to the foreigner hospital beds, I wanted out ASAP. Cuban medicine, I found out, was no more than animal husbandry. The doctors were paid one dollar per

day, their service was of no value, and because there was
no court system to address malpractice, there was no
incentive for professionalism.

Perry had gone straight into building two at La
Condesa. Building two was much more civilized than
buildings one and three. Perry had learned this before-
hand and refused to enter the other buildings. With
only thirty-six total prisoners housed in nine ten- by
twelve-foot rooms, it did not have the atmosphere of a
chicken coop. There was a television room in the front,
with a hallway running the length of the building in
front of the nine cells. The cell doors were never closed,
and it felt more like a college dormitory. With only four
men to a room, they didn't have to listen to the
cacophony of fifty to eighty prisoners. The kitchen in
the back had better ventilation, and the bathrooms and
showers were in much better condition. The toilets were
still holes in the floor, the rats could still come up while
you squatted over them, and they had their own flies by
the hundred — always the flies, always the sewer smell,
and when the wind was out of the west, the stench of
the pig farm that was a hundred yards behind the
prison. But all in all, out of the hundreds of thousands
of prisoners in Cuba, these thirty-six men had it the
best. I wanted to get into building two.

CHAPTER TWENTY-ONE

Perry was a petroleum engineer. He had been working in Cuba for a number of years through a Canadian oil services contractor. Perry was a generous man, and he had befriended a Cuban family. His contract allowed him to travel back to Canada numerous times a year. He would bring back gifts for the Cuban family and helped them in any way he could to make their life easier. The family had a teenage daughter, and the daughter had a friend that Perry had seen two or three times before. The fifteen-year-old friend's parents had found her with forty American dollars. Upon questioning, she told them that she was having sex with a foreigner. Her parents called the police, and the police investigation came to the conclusion that the only foreigner she knew was Perry King. Perry was questioned by the police, and he told them the few times he had seen the girl, it was always in the presence of the Cuban family. The date that the police told Perry the girl had earned the forty dollars as a prostitute, Perry had been in Canada for an extended stay. Perry felt he had nothing to fear and went about his business until two weeks later, when he was arrested. The company he worked for questioned the authorities about the validity of the arrest, and the police told them the girl had corrected her story and had been mistaken about the date of the occurrence. They also told the company that they had photos. Well, when the company heard that the police had photos as evidence, they apologized for questioning the validity of the arrest and abandoned Perry from that moment on. The Canadian embassy also was told that the police had photos as evidence and stopped its objections to his arrest. No one ever asked to see the photo evidence, because who wants to see a grown man having sex with a fifteen-year-old girl? It wasn't until Perry's one-hour court hearing that the photos were shown to be of a man pointing at the girl's bedroom window. The police had gotten this man to agree that he saw Perry and the girl having sex through this window. He did not have to testify in court, and no one knew who he was. The completely fabricated case resulted in a twenty-five-year sentence. Welcome to the Hotel Fidel Castro!

CHAPTER TWENTY-TWO

I t was about this time, in July 2003, as I waited for the paperwork that would tell me how many years in prison Fidel wanted of me, that I started singing this little verse to the tune of "Hotel California":

Welcome to the Hotel Fidel Castro
such an ugly place, such an ugly face
We're all locked up at the Hotel Fidel Castro
any time of year you can find us here
our minds are definitely twisted
but no Mercedes-Benz
there are lots of furry, furry rats
but we're not friends
relax in the prison cell, bunk full of sweat
some cry to remember, some cry to forget

I also learned how to go to sleep in my bunk sweating. We all had small fans blowing right on our bunk while we slept, but the air was so hot and humid, we would still fall asleep wiping the sweat from our face. About 4 a.m., the temperature would fall below a hundred degrees inside building three, and many men stayed up in the television room until then. They would sleep from 4 a.m. until 7 a.m., at which time we had to stand by our bunks to be counted. They would sleep three more hours until ten o'clock, when it was necessary to have all the beds made and everything in order for daily inspection. I had been a morning person for many years, so I forced myself to learn to fall asleep sweating rather than staring at a mindless Cuban television program half the night, because the light was turned off at 10 p.m.

The prison's light bulbs resembled Edison's first model. The glass was clear, but the filament was very weak, maybe fifteen watts. There were no light bulb sockets, but the Cubans had perfected a way to twist the bare wires around the bulb, not only powering it but also holding on to it. There was no way to read by them. Carmen had brought me a small battery-powered light that was made to clip onto a book. With it, I could read the old *International Herald Tribune* and magazines I purchased every month. There were a few books in English in the small prison library, so I read all those that I could. All the English books were brought by other prisoners, but it wasn't until Perry had his family start bringing him a suitcase full of books every three months that we had good books to read.

I had asked Carmen to bring me some music. Most of the men had CD players, which allowed them to listen to their favorite music, but I needed something to drown out the constant cacophony of the island boys all talking at once and as loud as possible. The music I wanted was from the early 1980s, and I didn't even know if it was available on CD. So I asked her to look in the cassette section of the music store for Black Sabbath's "Heaven and Hell" and Dio's "The Last in Line." She found them both for $1.99 each and brought along with them an old Sony Walkman. With the almost constant noise of the island boys screaming and yelling inside building three, I spent hours a day listening to Ronnie James Dio's lyrics and would apply them to the suffering and despair that I witnessed on a daily basis. Being lucky enough to be born in the United States and live a Peter Pan lifestyle up until this point was heaven. The Cubans' daily struggle for existence was hell in my eyes. Cuban prisoners were definitely the last in line when it came to handing out luck.

CHAPTER TWENTY-THREE

A few months earlier, three men from Curaçao showed up: Edgar, Dito and David. Dito and David were arrested for smuggling. In their interrogation, they were asked if they knew Edgar, and as Curaçao was a small island, they said yes. Dito was seventeen and David was twenty-one, and the criminal activity they were involved in had no connection to Edgar, who was the age of their grandparents. But state security had its eye on Edgar for a long time. Edgar's wife was Cuban, and he would travel to Cuba on a regular basis to bring necessities and gifts to his wife's family. He also became friendly with all their neighbors, handing out hundreds of dollars in cash per visit, as well as sponsoring a block party with music, rum and beer. Cuba was able to remove Edgar, his money and his parties for good. All it took was a simple fabrication of a connection to Dito and David. Curaçao was a Netherlands protectorate, and The Netherlands was making a lot of noise about the arrest of the seventy-five dissidents. Fidel thought he could stop that with the imprisonment of its citizens. It didn't.

Edgar had the bunk right next to mine. I had swapped bunks — for a fee, of course — so I was no longer next to Capt. Know-It-All. Edgar spoke five languages perfectly, and one of them was English. He was in his late fifties, had always lived life to the fullest and had a great sense of humor. We both saw humor in many of the same things. After hearing my story, we would roll with laughter making fun of Capt. Know-It-All. Edgar would become my best friend, and finding humor anywhere we could became essential to keeping our sanity.

Edgar also questioned me about the Ronnie James Dio lyrics I would utter from time to time. It wasn't long before he was making observations, applying Ronnie James Dio lyrics to them and then sharing them with me. He wasn't a fan of heavy rock music, but he understood the poetic nature of the words.

CHAPTER TWENTY-FOUR

Throughout my stay in Cuba's prisons, I refused to let my mother, sister and eldest brother visit me. I didn't want them to see me in such conditions. My mother's pleas on my behalf to various officials and agencies got nothing but sympathy in return.

"The small bits of information or hope she gets back from our government are only lip service," I wrote to my sister on September 23, 2003. "... Fact is this is the absolute worst time in history to be an American prisoner in Cuba. Carmen and I used to want to come sailing down here because we heard it was beautiful and friendly people. They have always had this Stalinist style police and court system, but they didn't put Americans through it. They just expelled them from the country. So we never heard about it, even in Key West."

In fact, some Americans who'd been caught with drugs in the past were sent home. Jerry was one of them. He'd been in and out of Marina Hemingway a couple of times. That's where he'd met Kevin. And on one of his trips, he had two pounds of marijuana hidden deep in the boat, in the bilge, when he docked in Cuba — his personal stash. As he recounted the story, he told officials that he'd forgotten the drugs were there. He spent two weeks in the box at Villa Marista before the police took him out, put him on his boat and told him not to come back.

Now, things were different. This month, prisoners who got their paperwork and hadn't believed prosecutors could get the twenty- to thirty-year sentences they sought returned from court with those very sentences. Lengthy prison terms were such a foregone conclusion, the court date resembled not a trial, but a sentencing hearing. Judges would either nod in agreement with the prisoners as Cuban lawyers argued for innocence or nod off in feigned sleep. The people who sat as judges were common citizens but smart enough to try to display their disassociation with the inevitable outcome of each hearing.

That's when our papers came. They described the facts with a certainty that only a police state could muster. Everything was as I expected, except the marijuana was listed as five hundred pounds now. Someone had made off with a hundred and fifty pounds of Jerry's weed. Fidel wanted to give Capt. Know-It-All and I thirty years in this communist gulag. I felt that thirty years in prison for my pseudo-intellectual idiot of a captain was fair. But for me? I was like all the other men who could not believe this was happening to them. Yes, most of them were either innocent or had the charges trumped up based on falsehoods and fabrication. But it wasn't my boat, and it wasn't my marijuana. I didn't know who the people were in Jamaica, nor who would get it in Florida. I had never made a dime from smuggling. I had never before been involved in any criminal activity. I had a bad driving record in the 1990s, but that was it. Way before I completed thirty years in the Hotel Fidel Castro, I would be dead. If it weren't for Paolo's plan, it was hopeless. Paolo's plan kept me from utter despair.

I had to try something. I started asking again about Cuban lawyers and the possibility of using money to get my mitigating circumstances considered. In conversation with Doc, he told me that he originally had gotten papers for a twenty-five year sentence. He was able to get fifteen hundred dollars to the prosecutor and five thousand dollars to his victim's family. He had already received new papers for a five-year sentence and at court would receive another two-year reduction. The convicted pedophile would serve only a three-year sentence, less with time off for good behavior. It didn't seem fair. His lawyer, as well as the other inquiries I had sent out, suggested that it wasn't possible for an American on smuggling charges to buy some justice. Thank God for Paolo's plan.

CHAPTER TWENTY-FIVE

This was the rainy season in Cuba, so while I waited for my court date, thunderstorms pounded La Condesa almost every day. The roof leaked in about ten places, so every afternoon we would move our bunks and have our buckets in place. Everyone had a cheap plastic bucket that we used to do laundry. With forty-seven men in building three, there was always someone doing their washing in the back. We had to wash all our own clothes as well as our bedding, sheets and towels. Some men would wash in the evening and then hang them on the line to dry in the morning; others would wash in the morning and hang them, but they all had to be off the line by one o'clock, when the rains started. No one mistook my clothes for anyone else's. My shirts all had the sleeves cut off.

The prison would turn the water off three times a day, usually in the late morning, the late afternoon and then at midnight, when the water would stay off until

6 a.m. Depending on our jailers' mood, sometimes it was off twenty minutes, or sometimes it was off four hours. If there was a fight among the prisoners, four hours. If Fidel came on the television and bad-mouthed the United States and Europe, four hours.

Except for the three winter months, the electricity would go off every day and sometimes twice a day. This was some kind of roving blackout to conserve electrical power across Cuba. It meant no electricity to run the well-water pump to fill the water tower, no electricity to run our fans that spared us from the 110-degree heat, no television for the simple-minded men, and no lights. We gringos who could afford to have battery chargers and spare batteries learned to prepare ourselves. Some of us even had battery-powered fans.

CHAPTER TWENTY-SIX

Besides the low-rank guards who would open and lock the doors, there were three prison officials we had to deal with on a daily basis. These Cuban men were from the department of the interior, which was also their Army. They lived like soldiers in barracks, ate the same crap food that we did and therefore were all skinny. Except for one. He was Capt. Sermiento, and he was a fat man. Sermiento was in charge of discipline and punishment. The other two officials, Daniel and one I called Mighty Mouse, were in charge of re-education.

Having these two young Cuban men in charge of re-educating me made me laugh with incredulity the first time I was seated before them. Every morning after inspection as we stood by our bunks, one of these three men would have a speech for us. One of the bilingual prisoners would be asked to translate for them, and we would stand there for twenty minutes listening to worthless information intertwined with communist dogma. At times the Colonel, who was the top official at La Condesa, would come in and give us a speech of exceptionally worthless information intertwined with colossal communist dogma. At times he would bring with him other high-ranking officials, as well as Cuban government officials, for them to view the nice collection of foreign hostages. We were made to stand there like some type of military parade while the generals and bureaucrats walked to and fro. There seemed to be an endless supply of Cuban officials visiting our chicken-coop prison. Maybe it was a pilgrimage that obedient and productive Cuban officials were granted, like going to a zoo, but more prestigious. And everyone wanted to make a speech. Even the hundreds of flies could not stop their speeches by flying into the mouth of the orator, speeches full of absurd communist brainwashing crap.

But as we struggled to survive with our sanity intact, laughter became an essential ingredient, and after the visits had finished, laugh we all did at the absurdity of these visit rituals. The prison officials and government officials were brainwashed in the righteousness of the revolution, and the common people were brainwashed in fear.

This evil, where does it come from? How did it get in Fidel Castro's head and suppress a whole nation, two generations of people that are capable of so much more than basic survival?

Take it like a man.

CHAPTER TWENTY-SEVEN

Sermiento came to building three one morning in late November 2003 and told Capt. Know-It-All and I to pack all our things and put them in front of building two. A couple of guys were congratulating me, thinking I was being moved to building two. But most of the guys, as well as myself, knew that we were going to Combinado del Este prison in Havana. It was not a surprise, because they had been sending the other men facing high prison sentences to Combinado just before they went to court and got their thirty-year sentences so they would be in a secure facility if they freaked out. The Big House! Cuba's showcase prison! I had been only to the hospital there but had heard about the conditions in the cellblocks from Perry and Sharkey.

At the main gate at Combinado, our possessions

were searched, we were strip-searched, and a woman counted my money five times. Four thousand dollars to a Cuban was a lifetime of wages. The Combinado del Este officials stood there and watched.

"You can have it all," I said to the one next to me, "just give me a ride to the airport."

"Como?" he responded. He didn't speak English.

My new jailers put me in the solitary confinement cell. After nine months at the chicken coop of La Condesa, it was a welcome change. I had all the stuff Carmen had brought me, some food, some smokes and some reading material. I was OK with it. They came and got me three days later and took me up to the fourth floor. Along the way, I passed large cells crammed with many Cuban men. This didn't look like a chicken coop. This was a rat cage full of human beings. As soon as I say hello to Sharkey and the other men I knew, I thought, I would do something to get sent back to solitary confinement.

On the fourth floor, we went around the corner to the back wing of the building. We passed small cells with two men apiece, and they all said hello as we passed. These guys looked as unhappy to be here as I was. They had the same look my face also wore, a look that said, "There must be some mistake." I would soon find out these men were among the seventy-five dissidents arrested the previous spring. At the end of the hall, a sign had been painted that said "special area" in

Spanish. Through another gate, I found Sharkey and twenty other foreign prisoners housed in five cells. Their cell doors were all open, and there was a central TV room, a wide hallway and vertical prison windows with a commanding view of the Cuban countryside.

CHAPTER TWENTY-EIGHT

The prison officials, my new re-educators, put Capt. Know-It-All and myself in the same cell. That had to change. I could not stand to see his face or hear his voice any more than necessary. The cells had four racks, with three bunks on each one. The bottom bunk was about six inches off the floor, and the top bunk more than six feet in the air. I didn't even pick one, because I wasn't staying.

Of the four other men already in the cell, one of them was called Bella. He was originally from India but had been living in Bolivia for a number of years. He spoke English, and I had many conversations with him when he was at La Condesa six months previously. He was a gracious and well-spoken man, but while at La Condesa he lost his temper and told the re-educators what he honestly thought of Cuba and the revolution. If a prisoner had any hope of getting by, he couldn't do that. As an enemy of the revolution, Bella would never go back to La Condesa. As a matter of fact, he would go on to tell the Combinado re-educators what he thought of them, Cuba and the revolution. One couldn't do that either. He was moved from the Big House to the lowest communist gulag for foreign prisoners, a rat cage called Guanajay.

Kaiser was also here. Kaiser was from Tanzania. I had first seen Kaiser back at La Condesa when I arrived there. He acted kind of crazy then, and sure enough, while at La Condesa, he cut his wrists with the single, no-handle razor blades they issued to all prisoners for shaving. That got him an immediate trip to Combinado del Este, and he had been here since. But he had gotten a whole lot crazier. He would sit in the same chair for eighteen hours and not move. He always had a blanket wrapped around him, and no one could tell that he was pissing himself. He sat there so long, by the time he had gotten up, it was dry. People would ask Kaiser to bathe until the time he was found inside the barrel of water that we used not just to pour over our head for bathing, but for drinking. Kaiser had received his sentence of twenty-four years for smuggling by making the mistake of changing airplanes in Cuba. Two years after his arrest, he was sent home to Tanzania, judged to be mentally ill. I later learned that just before Kaiser was taken to the airport, he confessed to the other men that he had been acting crazy for the whole two years just so he could be released early. He had been accused of play-acting from time to time but would never admit it. When any Cubans were around, he played a hundred percent crazy. Through the years, I often wondered if I could have done that. I don't think so. I feel I survived by wearing indignation and disgust on my face every time I was in front of a Cuban official.

Sharkey was in the first cell with two Bahamians. One was an eighteen-year-old called Blitz and the other a Rastafarian named Derek. Being in the same cell as Sharkey would not be pleasant. He would start talking and never shut up, but most of his chatter was hilarious, whether it was true or bullshit. The Bahamians seemed pretty cool, so I got the re-educators to approve my move to Derek's cell. Derek was so cool, in fact, that to this day, he is the coolest person I have ever met.

CHAPTER TWENTY-NINE

Derek, whom we called Rasta, was a Bahamian with a prosperous smuggling career until he got bold and took a boat full of marijuana across the Gulf Stream. It was seized in South Florida. He was taken to Miami Metropolitan jail, where the next morning he was led to a room to await his arraignment hearing. His jailer took off one cuff of the handcuffs and locked it to the small metal chair where he'd seated Rasta and left the room. Obviously, Rasta was still feeling bold, because with his long Rastafarian finger-nails, he was able to unscrew a bolt in the chair. He slipped the handcuff down the chair leg and off, climbed through a one-foot-square window near the ceiling and fell almost three stories into the bushes outside.

He ran for four blocks, found a taxicab, explained

that he had just been mugged and beaten and asked for a ride to the airport. He took the driver's name and said he would be back within a week to give him a hundred dollars for the ride. No problem, the driver said.

Inside the Bahamasair terminal, with a face cut and bloody from his fall, he was able to hide the handcuffs under the sleeve of his shirt on one wrist as he explained to his countrymen at the counter that he had been mugged and beaten. His family in the Bahamas would pay for the ticket upon his arrival, he said. No problem, he was told; the next flight would leave in fifteen minutes. About thirty minutes after falling out of the window at the Miami Metropolitan jail, he was in the air on his way to Nassau. A little paranoia in this situation was appropriate, so when the plane landed and turned off the runway to taxi to the terminal, Rasta made sure he was the first one out the door and ran not to the terminal, but to the fence in the opposite direction. He got out of there and on a boat back to his home island.

Feeling insecure about the Drug Enforcement Agency's ability to reach into the Bahamas and pluck anyone they wanted, he left the islands and went to Europe for a number of years. When he felt it was safe to return to the Bahamas, he did so. It wasn't. He was arrested and put in jail in Nassau, awaiting extradition to the United States. He spent three years in jail in the Bahamas fighting extradition and won. He won because he had not been arraigned in court for the crime of smuggling; the only crime they had against him was eluding a corrections officer, which was not an extra-ditable offense. American law enforcement knew that to be the case all along but was able to ring three years of Fox Hill prison degradation out of Rasta's spirit.

Rasta had only been out for three months when he found himself in Jamaica with a pocket full of money to buy himself a good boat. Unfortunately, he met another Rastafarian friend who already had a boat full of dope that needed new engines. He talked Rasta into buying the engines with the promise of repaying him fivefold in the Bahamas.

These island boys, half of them Jamaican, the others Bahamian, were all children of the sea, but their boating skills could not save them from being washed up on the shore of Cuba. Rasta would spend nine years in the Hotel Fidel Castro for a total of twelve years in prison. If he had not climbed out the window but had acquiesced to justice in the United States, he would have been deported after three years or so.

CHAPTER THIRTY

There was a telephone in the hallway for our use. The Cubans would turn it on and off at will. Since it was on and I had stashed away some telephone cards, I called the U.S. Interests Section and told the officials there of the prison change: Hotel Fidel Castro, Big House. They seem shocked that we would be moved without their notification, but there was nothing they could do. I also called Carmen and gave her the new telephone number.

As I was speaking to Carmen, the re-educators came, took me off the phone and marched Capt. Know-It-All and myself down to the first floor. There I found more prison officials and two young Cuban women in their twenties. They were our court-appointed lawyers. There wasn't a translator present, but we were motioned to sign some papers. This was the one and only pre-court-date meeting we would have with our lawyers. We didn't exchange a word. Court was four days away.

We were to be taken back to Hotel Fidel Castro downtown to be close to the courthouse. I spent the next three days writing and revising a fifteen-minute plea for mercy. The outcome was a foregone conclusion, but I thought maybe, if it was my lucky day, I could get my sentence below twenty years. I might survive that. No way could I survive thirty years.

I had some decent clothes, but they were in storage outside the prison gates, and I was not able to retrieve them. I was taken back to Villa Marista for one night in the box with no clothes other than my worn gym shorts and T-shirt. The next morning in the holding cell at the courthouse, I was still revising my statement, and Capt. Know-It-All told me that I shouldn't admit guilt because he had sent letters to various important people in the United States saying he'd had only a couple of ounces of marijuana. Yeah, right! A delusional pseudo-intellectual. When I was taken into the courtroom, I felt like a totalitarian police state prisoner, and I'm sure that's exactly what I looked like. I recognized one of the two Americans there from the U.S. Interests Section, two gringo spectators in a donkey court.

CHAPTER THIRTY-ONE

There were five judges, and none of them looked happy to be there. The prosecutor was a woman in her mid-forties, and she looked delighted that this day had finally come. A young woman who was the translator came and introduced herself and briefly explained how the proceedings would go. We were told we could refuse to testify, or we had the option of making a statement, with or without the prosecutor asking us questions. Capt. Know-It-All told the prosecutor he wouldn't be saying anything, and I told her I would like to make a statement but felt no advantage to answering the prosecutor's questions.

All of the judges were in their fifties or sixties and appeared to be average citizens, not ex-lawyers. As the prosecutor presented her case, they seemed uninterested or nodded off to sleep. When my interrogator from a year ago finished making his statement, my lawyer asked him if we had cooperated during the investigation. He said, yes, at all times. My lawyer seemed pleased, as if that should deserve some leniency. She obviously didn't know how powerful the box was in inducing cooperation. During my fifteen-minute plea for mercy, not one of the judges would look me in the eye. After three hundred and sixty-two days since arriving at Marina Hemingway, the proceedings were over in about an hour and a half. The Cubans had secured their totalitarian police state justice. There was nothing left but the crying. Cry, cry, cry.

In the police car ride back to Combinado prison, it was obvious that Capt. Know-It-All was not happy with my mea culpa and plea for mercy. I was quite happy to have that whole process over with. During the twenty-minute ride to Hotel Fidel Castro, Big House, I had to laugh out loud at the thought of Capt. Know-It-All being so delusional as to believe his letters to important Americans could save him from our fate.

Upon returning to the Big House, we were welcomed back by the members of the "special area." Everyone wanted to know how the court appearance went. Everyone who had not been to court yet still held out hope that they might get a fair trial. What I went through was not a trial at all but a sentencing hearing, and I told them so. But I was an American. America is Fidel's enemy. Surely he would not be as harsh on them.

I had thought about everyone being Fidel's hostages, but it wasn't yet conclusive in my mind. These other guys held out hope that their cases were only misunderstandings or that they would receive a short sentence for their insignificant smuggling activity.

CHAPTER THIRTY-TWO

Two of the men in the "special area" were young Russian guys. They were hoping their case would be found to be a misunderstanding. Dimitri and Rudy had been changing planes at Havana airport and traveling with one other Russian, Peter. As with all the men I have met here, they were coming from Latin America and just changing planes here on their way to Europe. As customs searched their luggage, they found dope in Peter's suitcase. "It's not mine," Peter had told them, pointing at Rudy. Rudy echoed Peter and said it was Dimitri's. Dimitri and Rudy had made the good decision not to smuggle dope to Europe but did not concern themselves with Peter's activity. Yet all three of them got the same sentence, thirty years each.

The cell that I bunked in with Sharkey, Rasta and

Blitz was a larger version of the box. About four times the size of the box and designed for twelve men, it was downright roomy with only four of us. It also had a shower stall separate from the hole-in-the-floor toilet. The shower stall did not have its own water pipe. One water pipe worked, and it was turned on once a day to fill a rusted barrel that served all our water needs. Everyone used plastic soda bottles to catch drinking water as it came out of the pipe. It had to be cleaner than the water sitting in the rusty barrel, right? It didn't matter much. If the water didn't make you sick, the food was going to make you sick. No one was ever, ever constipated. We would use this barrel water to brush our teeth, pour on our head with a large cup for a shower, and flush the hole in the floor with a bucket. But we could never flush the smell of the hole in the floor.

I settled into a daily routine awaiting word of my fate: a stale piece of bread with bone juice in the morning; cards or backgammon with Rasta, Sharkey and Bella; then crap for lunch. The afternoon meant more cards with the boys and crap for dinner. Rasta wouldn't eat anything except the vegetables, which were few and far between. Just about everything else in Cuba was cooked with pig fat. Rastafarians don't eat pig. I ate everything, not caring what it did to my stomach. I was always hungry, but Rasta was starving. Sharkey was always droning on with some absurd story, but it helped keep my mind off the impending notice of doom I was to receive. It came six days later. Everyone said it had come in record time; most waited one to two months for their sentences.

The re-educators came and got Capt. Know-It-All and myself, took us around the corner past the dissidents, with their expressions of shock still on their faces, and down to an unused dining room with concrete tables and concrete benches. There were waiting two men and a woman. The woman's English was as bad as my Spanish, and she introduced the men as judges in our case. We were now to be the first prisoners to receive our sentence in person. It was great to be an American in Cuba.

She started translating into English our sentence papers, and I felt building in me the need to choke somebody to death. The only thing that stopped me was that I couldn't decide who to choke first, Capt. Know-It-All or one of the Cubans. What I needed was Fidel Castro's skinny old neck in my hands. Capt. Know-It-All received his thirty-year sentence, and I received five years off for my courtroom speech. A merciful sentence of twenty-five years in the Hotel Fidel Castro. As we were led back to our cells, I'm sure the dissidents recognized the expression on my face as that on their own.

The phone had been turned off since the day before Christmas and would stay off. I could not call the Interests Section nor Carmen to get an appeal process started. An appeal had to be filed within ten days. The phone came back on eleven days later.

I was constantly on the phone, complaining to the Interests Section or to Carmen. Within a couple of days of me ranting and raving to Carmen, the Cubans had pulled her phone number and would not allow my calls to be completed to her. We knew that the Cubans monitored all our phone calls, but I guess they decided that my calls to Carmen contained too many facts and too much truth. I was able to send a message to Carmen to get a different cell phone number, and by the time she had done so, it was all over but the crying. I would not be able to communicate and file a appeal in the ten days required to do so. Take it like a man!

That winter of 2003 seemed very cold. Only about three cold fronts a year in Cuba are strong enough to lower the temperature into the forties. Maybe it was because we were on the fourth floor, where the wind would howl through and leave me shivering in my bunk at night. We would sleep with our clothes on at night, as well as a blanket, but when it was forty-five degrees outside, it was also forty-five degrees in our cell. It seems that my body had absolutely no resistance to the cold. Possibly it was the protein-free diet they served us. I had heard that the Cuban prisoners here at Combinado del Este received half the amount of food we did. Someone mentioned that Cubans eat half our amount of prison food their whole life, not just in prison. I just couldn't imagine how the other ten thousand prisoners here at the Big House would have the will to cling to life, half-starved and half freezing.

"They cling to hope because they think the United States is going to save them. George Bush Junior is coming!" Sharkey said. "I kid you not."

"Forget it, Sharkey," I said, laughing.

CHAPTER THIRTY-THREE

On the fourth floor, we looked out toward the prison hospital and over the roof of the prison kitchen. Beyond the kitchen was the prison fence, then the Cuban countryside on a rising hill, its crest about a quarter-mile away from us. This scrubland seemed to be used as pasture for cattle, except for a small patch of sugarcane that Sharkey had once tried to convince me was full-grown medical-grade marijuana. We could watch the Cuban prisoners who worked in the kitchen load up small barrels of the slop onto flatbed trucks that was delivered as our food. We could also see the prisoners mow the grass alongside the fence as well as two of the guard towers.

One day, as another card game progressed with Sharkey, Rasta, Bella and myself, we heard two fire-cracker sounds.

"Those were gunshots," Sharkey said.

You can't believe Sharkey, but he bolted to the windows with the rest of us right behind him. At the fence halfway between the two guard towers was a grass-mowing prisoner with a pair of wire cutters in his hand. He was looking at the guard tower but frozen in place. All of us foreigners were now at the window and waiting for the guards to come and get him. Five seconds passed, and he resumed cutting the fence. Four more shots rang out, each spaced about one second apart, but we could see the dirt flying ten yards on either side of the prisoner. The guards were shooting short on purpose so as not to hit the prisoner, and he just kept cutting the wire. All of us at the fourth floor window started cheering at the top of our lungs. Quite soon we were all in sync, yelling, "Go! Go! Go!"

And go he did. He finished cutting a hole in the fence and climbed through. Two more shots rang out. But both of these were ten yards short as well. He ran twenty yards and was into the brush. We continued to scream, "Go! Go! Go!" while scanning the hillside, trying to pick up his path. A prisoner trusted enough to have that job close to the fence had planned this out and knew where he was going. He would have to veer to the left on the hillside to stay under the cover of brush for two hundred yards, so he could cross the crest of the hill unseen.

Five minutes later, we were still cheering, and the

first guard on the ground showed up with a dog, but inside the fence. The dog didn't want to go through that slender cut in the fence, nor did the guard. Five minutes after that, seven guards appeared on the far side of the fence and fanned out up the hillside. Two of the guards had dogs but would not release them to follow the scent. Possibly Cuban guard dogs were not trained to follow a scent. At the same time, five guards appeared on the crest of the hill a quarter-mile away, spread out and scanning the hillside back toward the prison. By then, our re-educators had appeared on the fourth floor and locked all of us in our cells. By now, our cheering and chanting had turned to hilarious laughter and ridicule of Cuban tactics. By climbing on the unused third-level bunks, we could still watch their futile actions. Thirty minutes after the prisoner escaped, someone in charge out there decided to set fire to the brush and burn him out. They must have used plenty of gasoline, because within five minutes, the whole hillside was on fire.

Outside of the prison fence on the hillside was the prison auto shop and garage. As with most old garages, there were old junk vehicles in the back. Here were about three cars, four trucks and two old yellow school buses, all with tall weeds growing through them. With the wind blowing fifteen miles an hour from left to right, we all started chanting, "Bus! Bus! Bus!" We were not to be denied. A ten-foot wall of fire hit the school buses and the other vehicles while we in our cells danced, laughed and traded high-fives as they burned.

The re-educators came back and gave us a five-minute communist speech and a hint of severe punishment to come. No one cared. We were ecstatic with joy for the Cuban prisoner who got away from the Hotel Fidel Castro, Big House. We never saw him again.

CHAPTER THIRTY-FOUR

W e were locked in our cells most of the time for the next week. They would let us out to watch television in the evening. I never cared to watch the communist crap, except when Fidel Castro was talking. One evening during his routine roundtable speeches, he started speaking of the insolence of the younger generation. He said if they were not willing to become good socialists on their own, he had a place for them. Our prisons are like universities, he said. We will teach them to be good socialists. Everyone in the TV room who understood Spanish cracked up laughing, and when we gringos got the translation, we did so as well. But then the discussion turned to how could this happen in the 21st century, ninety miles from the United States of America. How could people go to prison for not believing in a political system long ago shown to be nothing but mental and physical slavery? The one question all the men had for me: Why won't the United States do something about it?

One day we noticed from our fourth-floor windows that many workmen and prisoners had begun scurrying, working like there was no tomorrow. Men replaced windows and painted the hospital and the front side of all three prisoner buildings. Others carried in new flooring material, doors, beds and equipment. Others re-sodded the grass in front of the hospital, planting palm trees and other plants. The work went on twenty-four hours a day for ten days, by the glow of spotlights at night. We knew someone was coming, but we were amazed at how much our jailers had planned on impressing their visitors. I found out from our consulate that Fidel Castro had been criticized for the treatment of the seventy-five dissidents as well as prisoners in general. For the first time ever, the Cubans were going to allow United Nations officials and reporters from the outside world to see one of their prisons and talk to prisoners.

We knew they weren't going to let them talk to us up here in the "special area," and the next day, when the visitors arrived, we were all locked down in our cells. The visitors got a carefully choreographed tour and were presented with Cuban prisoners who praised the officials for allowing them three meals a day and the ability to work in the hospital and train as a nurse. They weren't allowed to open any doors or go where they wanted to go, nor were they allowed to talk to foreigners or political prisoners. These Western reporters knew what was going on, and they wrote as much in their stories. The U.S. diplomat was able to slip me a couple of photocopies of their stories on his next visit. We found it amazing that the Cuban officials were so clueless as to think they could spend all that money and all that time creating a façade that fooled no one. But then, their whole communist system was a façade that only fooled themselves.

CHAPTER THIRTY-FIVE

Carmen had been wanting to come and visit for two months, but I kept putting her off, asking her to wait until I was transferred back to La Condesa. I finally relented, and in late March, she arrived for a one-week visit. She brought me a suitcase full of things that made my Combinado stay much less torturous. We had one four-hour conjugal visit together on Monday, but they refused to let her visit me again for the remainder of the week. We were never given a reason for denying us additional visits, and every attempt by me or Carmen to find out why went nowhere. That was the beginning of the end for our relationship. She spent the rest of that week in her downtown Havana hotel room.

Carmen is of Puerto Rican descent, so she could pass for a Cuban. One day, she returned to her hotel after an outing. Hotel security stopped her in the lobby and asked her where she thought she was going. She didn't know it was hotel security, because all state security in Cuba is undercover. Carmen, in turn, wanted to know who the hell would ask her such a question. She went into a tirade of yelling and insulted body language worthy of any Puerto Rican woman on Earth. Finally, with a large enough crowd of managers and security, she told them that she was not a stinking Cuban but was a guest in the hotel from the United States. Cubans were not allowed to enter any of the hotels designated for foreigners, just as slaves were not allowed to enter the owner's house two hundred years ago unless they worked in it.

CHAPTER THIRTY-SIX

The following week, twelve of us were told by the re-educators to pack our things. We would be going to La Condesa the following morning. We went nowhere the following morning but kept our bags packed for two weeks, waiting for the moment to leave Combinado prison. I finally realized this was just another exercise in psychological torture, similar in effect as making Carmen wait five days for another visit with me that never came. I unpacked my things and settled back into the same daily routine. The next day, the Colonel came from La Condesa prison and had us all assembled together in the unused dining room so he could give us a one-hour, communist, smoke-up-our-ass speech. He ended his oral gift of enlightenment by saying eight prisoners would return to La Condesa the following morning. His statement turned out to be true.

I envisioned leaving Capt. Know-It-All there at Combinado prison to continue suffering the depravity that he richly deserved. But there is no God in Cuba, only a wizard named Fidel Castro. I said goodbye to Sharkey, Bella, Russians Dimitri and Rudy, as well as Kaiser and the rest of the men, and we left, with Capt. Know-It-All in tow.

Upon arriving at La Condesa, both Capt. Know-It-All and I were put into building one, also known as the ghetto: eighty men all living like rats in a box, stacked on top of one another. The feng shui was atrocious. Building three was full at the time, but since I had my refrigerator there, I would be the first person to be moved when a bunk became available. Alex, the "girl" from Columbia, was in building one, so I hired him to wash all my clothes and bedding to remove the barrel-water smell of Combinado del Este.

Building one housed seventy men with no financial help from home. They were all looking for some work to make a little money so they could eat better. I hired someone to cook for me and started putting back on the twenty-five pounds I had lost at the Big House. Eight days later, a bunk became available in building three. I moved back, leaving Capt. Know-It-All to suffer in building one. Kevin would be stuck there for two years. Nine years would've been better.

Building one was twice as bad as building three, but I set about trying to get into building two, which was by far the most civilized chicken coop at La Condesa. This was the summer of 2004, and the consul from the U.S. Interests Section would come to La Condesa for a visit every three months. A Cuban man from their Foreign Ministry would monitor our conversations. He was a very gracious older black man, and during both visits that summer, I spoke directly to him concerning my desire to be in building two. Prison officials, who were also in the room monitoring our conversation, gave me dirty looks each time I addressed the issue to him. But three days after the visit of August 2004, I was told to pack my things and move to building two.

Building two was divided into nine cells with a wide hallway running down the side of them. There were cell doors, but they were always pushed back against the wall. There were four men to a cell for a total of thirty-six men in the same size building as one and three, each with eighty men and forty-seven men, respectively. Each cell in building two was large enough to accommodate a table and had its own sink, as well. The cooking area in the back was well ventilated, and the bathrooms and showers were in much better condition, damn near civilized; feng shui, much better.

CHAPTER THIRTY-SEVEN

Monir was from Istanbul but had been in Aruba selling leather products to the tourists that his family made back in Turkey. Business had not been good, and like all of us prisoners in Cuba, he'd made a strategic error in judgment. He took the money he had accumulated and found a Colombian man who was willing to haul dope in his suitcase to Europe. While changing planes at Havana, everyone is required to go through Cuban customs, and although he had an ingenious way of hiding the dope, his hired mule started sweating profusely when they searched his suitcase. It took the Cuban customs man four searches to find it, and as soon as he did, Monir bolted out the airport door, running to catch a taxi on the main avenue a quarter-mile away. He was able to elude capture for three months by moving from rented room to rented room in Havana. He had someone from Turkey bring him twelve thousand dollars to buy an inflatable boat and motor so he could escape to the Florida Keys.

The person who arranged the purchase insisted on going as well, with family members coming along. In Cuba, someone always talks, and on the night of departure, the police were waiting for them at the seashore. They put everyone in vehicles but Monir. He bent down to tie his shoelaces and sprung from this sprinter's stance, running into the brush. He spent another twenty-four hours in the brush before coming face-to-face with a German shepherd police dog. With cuts and bruises all over his body and face from the branches, exhausted from his ordeal, a dog ready to take a bite out of him, he was captured. If only Monir had known that his friend could have taken ten thousand dollars to Miami and purchased a ride on the next boat of Brothers to the Rescue, or as Castro called them, human traffickers.

CHAPTER THIRTY-EIGHT

Walter was an American who grew up in Miami, surrounded by the Cuban exile community. He must've been kooky his whole life, because he gave all of a large inheritance to his local church and became active in the anti-Castro movement. One day in the mid-1990s, he decided to lead a one-man invasion of Cuba on his jet ski. He marched around Havana waving an American flag, put some crazy glue in the door locks of government buildings and caught the attention of Cuban state security. Once in the custody of state security, he let his imagination run wild. He told them of all of his tentative plans to take Cuba back from the Castros, real or imagined. His tales were so imaginative that the Cubans were convinced they had a terrorist in their custody and proceeded to torture him like one. Electrical shocks to the testicles and everything else that Stalin had passed down through the years of communist paranoia were applied to Walter. He got a life sentence, reduced to twenty-five years on appeal, evidently because someone got a psychiatrist involved who said he was crazy. But that didn't matter; he was Fidel's Enemy No. 1. Walter had worn an old army surplus green shirt with ridiculous patches sewn onto it, and it had ended up in Fidel's museum of the revolution.

He was in building two at La Condesa when I got there. Everyone tiptoed around Walter because he was so volatile, and no one wanted to set him off. After an Italian broke his nose in building two, they moved him to one of the beds in the infirmary. Here they could load him up with antipsychotic pills, tranquilizers, and sedatives until he was up to twelve pills a day. I would try to go by at least once a day to say hello and chat with Walter so he wouldn't feel so isolated. The drugs they were giving him had a cumulative effect, and I watched Walter deteriorate over five years to a man who would not live much longer. I started telling the consuls when they would visit every three months of his worsening condition, and they wanted to see Walter themselves. But Walter had refused to see them for the last ten years because he had felt betrayed by the United States government. Finally, they sent Bonito the Cuban, with whom he had spoken on the telephone over the years. Bonito was able to confirm that this was a human being wrecked in body and spirit who would perish soon if his prison sentence continued. No one believed that Fidel would let his American terrorist go free. But he did. Besides, he had five other American hostages. When Walter walked out the gate of La Condesa, all one hundred eighty prisoners clapped and cheered at the sight no one ever thought would happen.

CHAPTER THIRTY-NINE

Maurice was a Canadian in his mid-seventies who had been given a seven-year sentence for marrying a Cuban woman a third his age. She was of legal age, but Maurice was a little on the mentally unstable side. He did not foresee that their age difference and him showering her and her family with gifts and money would raise the attention of state security. When she delivered his baby boy, government officials refused to put his name on the birth certificate as father. Being kind of kooky, he thought the name was important and started ranting and raving. His protests got him thrown in jail with a bogus criminal charge that led to at least a three-year stay at the Hotel Fidel Castro.

Maurice, always with a positive attitude, took his prison sentence well. He was in great physical condition for a man of his age. Most mornings he would call his young Cuban wife on the telephone and then, with a spring in his step, walked for two hours around the prison yard and did pull-ups in between his laps. "I spoke to my honey today," he'd often say, "so it's a beautiful day." He looked forward to the day that she could travel from south Cuba to visit him at La Condesa. When that day arrived, he was told by the officials that he could have only a sitting-room visit. No conjugal visit was allowed for Maurice. After that day, his attitude changed to one of hate for all the Cuban officials, regardless of whether they were responsible for his fate.

His health began to deteriorate, as his days were filled with combativeness and belligerence, a formula unlikely to yield an early release in Fidel's police state. His health became so bad that he had numerous trips to the prison hospital at Combinado. On one such trip, he was belligerent about his lack of care at the hospital and refused to get into the paddy wagon for the return trip to La Condesa. Four guards picked the seventy-four-year-old man up and literally threw him inside the paddy wagon head-first. His head crashed against the far wall. Maurice told me this himself but would tell me no more of what happened. When I asked the other men who were in the paddy wagon, they refused to discuss it. They were all fearful that the same thing could happen to them.

Maurice lay in one of the six beds of the La Condesa

infirmary complaining about neck pain and wanting to see a doctor. At that time, a young intern doctor would stop by La Condesa once a week but did nothing for Maurice. They thought he was faking it. About a month later, the staff decided Maurice needed to go to the hospital. Cuban Joe was one of the men asked to carry Maurice to the paddy wagon, and afterward, he said Maurice had been dead for a long time. Rigor mortis had already set in. The prison and officials told us the next day that Maurice had died in the middle of the night. The Cuban autopsy report showed death by natural causes. Every death that occurs in the Hotel Fidel Castro is by natural causes.

CHAPTER FORTY

Every night at eight o'clock or so, the guard would unlock the door and announce it was time for evening medication. In each building, there were at most six or seven prisoners that were on prescription medication they needed to receive from the nurse's station. But in the summer, it was so hot in our chicken coops, at least twenty men would go out the door just to get a breath of fresh air and wait in line for an aspirin at the nurse's station. Monir and I would always go out, and this one time I was commenting on the beauty of a potted palm tree outside the nurses' station. It was only a foot tall, but it looked exactly like a full-grown palm tree, almost as if it were a dwarf plant. Monir agreed and said if I would water it and make sure it had a bigger pot, giving it room to grow, in fifteen years I would be able to put my plastic chair underneath and sit in its shade for ten more years, implying that I would be here all that time. We both laughed, but maybe he was right. And I needed a hobby anyway. But not horticulture. I paid the nurse to water it.

Nazir had been in the business of helping people migrate from one country to another for many years. His Oxford education, ability to speak many languages, calm demeanor and generous smile allowed his uninterrupted success. He had helped rescue many Cubans and get them on the path to freedom in the United States. He had not worked in Cuba since two years previously, but his name had surfaced in another investigation by the Cuban police, and on his next trip to Cuba to visit friends, he found himself at Villa Marista, the Cuban name for Hotel Fidel Castro, Downtown. His interrogator was not able to make Nazir confess after two months. But the Cuban police imagination has an immense ability to run wild. The police came to the conclusion that Nazir was most likely a Pakistani terrorist. They could not get him to confess to terrorism, either, but they tried for eight more months. Finally, they fabricated a human trafficking charge and sent him to La Condesa. Nazir had spent one year in the box. When he arrived at La Condesa and told his story, everyone was in awe that he could survive for so long. He could barely walk and looked twenty years older than his true age, but his mind was sharp, and he was happy to see daylight for the first time in over a year.

CHAPTER FORTY-ONE

Starting in early 2004, there had been rumors that Fidel Castro was going to free all the foreign prisoners. It would be the right thing to do. No one deserved the long sentences they were facing, was the prevailing wishful thinking. People speculated that Castro was concerned that Hugo Chavez would lose his referendum that August and Cuba would be on its own again. In addition, everyone expected George W. Bush to lose his reelection bid to John Kerry, and Fidel wanted to start a clean slate with a Democratic president.

By August, even prison officials were dropping hints. "We have a big surprise for you," they'd say, or "We hope you will all be home with your family soon," and "We are so happy for you." Some men were selling their possessions, everything from plastic tables to cooking pots and pans. Hugo Chavez won his referendum,

George W. Bush won his reelection, but hope dies hard. Four months later, officials were still hinting there would be a big prison release, and two months after that, many prisoners still had their luggage packed, ready to go. It wasn't going to happen. Fidel Castro didn't need any consideration from the Western world, which was still giving him grief about the seventy-five dissidents locked up in prison.

CHAPTER FORTY-TWO

By January 2005, it was obvious that Carmen was drifting away and had no intention of returning to visit me. A Colombian guy named Sergio, who gave English and Spanish classes to the prisoners, had insight into what my Puerto Rican girlfriend required. The Latin lover explained that if I wanted her to come and visit me again, I needed to express my love for her. Sergio was also artistic and made custom greeting cards with his art supplies. He had three Spanish-language greeting cards, all complete with lengthy love poems. He suggested to motivate Carmen to come and visit, we needed to send all three. Carmen was shocked to receive a love poem from me, but the first one got her attention. The second one worked so well, she began making plans to come to Cuba in June. The third hand-drawn card I sent had her contacting Paolo the Brazilian to confirm the possibility of using his unused escape plan. He told her it could still be done, and she would give me the details when she came to Cuba in June. My original intention was just to motivate Carmen to visit me so I could have a week's worth of sex and two suitcases full of badly needed free-world supplies. It was a bonus that I now had renewed hope of getting out of here.

When she arrived, I surprised myself at how happy I was to see her. I had only seen her four hours in the last year and a half. I had forgotten what it was like to have real human contact, not just the day-to-day coexistence of my fellow prisoners. She explained how Paolo's plan would be accomplished, and I felt the thrill of excitement that it could be done. Even though I was in prison because I had been protecting Carmen, I did not ask her to use her own money for the cost of the operation. Before leaving Key West, she said she would get me out of jail if something went wrong, but I didn't hold her to that, because I felt she was more important now to act as a go-between with Paolo and my family. I knew my mother would never finance such a risky endeavor, so my plan was to have Carmen communicate with my sister and brother. Knowing the plan, they could present it as a lower-risk operation to my mother. My mother could afford it, a wealthy uncle could afford it, and if those failed, I felt that Carmen and her family would spring for it.

CHAPTER FORTY-THREE

In August 2005, the consul came to La Condesa for his scheduled visit. Whether it was a U.S. visit or any other country's, the prison officials always cleared out the guards from the administration buildings on the north side of the compound. It was as if they were trying to fool the diplomats into believing that La Condesa was a nice place because there were no guards in sight. We had noticed this years before, and it always amused prisoners that they would hide the guards from the diplomats.

There was a vehicle gate at the entrance, with a half-acre of parklike setting between it and the administration building where the consul would leave his vehicle. By parklike setting, I mean Cuban style, mostly concrete with small patches of grass. For this one visit, the prison official decided to have us wait on a concrete bench in the park area. The official told Cuban Joe to keep an eye on us, but Cuban Joe went in to see the consul first. That left Capt. Know-It-All, Dillon Jordan and myself sitting in the park alone, as planned, with no guards in sight. The consul's Suburban had been backed in toward the building and was pointing straight at the gate thirty yards away. The gate stood completely open, the Suburban's engine was running for the air-conditioning to keep the vehicle cool, and the little elderly Cuban man who was the driver was outside cleaning the windows.

Capt. Know-It-All spoke first. "Is this some kind of a test?"

Five minutes went by, with still no guards in sight and the gate wide open. Dillon Jordan always thought that he would be released at any moment, so he would not have considered jumping in that vehicle.

"I'd like to try it just to see how far I could get," Capt. Know-It-All said.

For myself, I had thought every day about what point of the fence would be best to go over. For two years, I had a hundred dollars in cash and forty dollars in international telephone cards hidden in my wallet for just this type of occasion. The only thing I lacked was a map. I had no idea where I was or which way to go. With the phone cards, I could call Carmen; she would make the connection in Miami with Cuban-Americans to have me hidden until the next available speedboat came to rescue some Cubans, and I would be on it, all for about fifteen thousand dollars. Definitely cheaper than Paolo's plan, but with more risk.

The little driver moved to the far side of the vehicle to clean those windows, and I felt myself putting pressure on the balls of my feet. My hamstrings started to tighten. It was a compulsion I had to fight with all my mental strength. Carmen had been here just two months ago and was finalizing the plan with Paolo back in Florida. Dillon Jordan would go in next to see the consul. Twenty minutes later, Capt. Know-It-All went in, and I was left there to watch that idling Suburban pointed toward the open gate for another ten minutes. Not one guard appeared the whole forty-five minutes of my wait. When my name was called to enter, I felt an emptiness inside me, thinking I had not accepted a gift from God.

After Carmen returned to the United States, I spent the next four months waiting every day for the plan to be finalized. No one would provide the twenty-five thousand dollars required up front. Paolo had said the balance could be paid when I was back in the United States. Two months after I had given up, my sister said she had the money available. By then it was too late. Paolo was nowhere to be found, and Carmen seemed to have lost interest in having me home.

CHAPTER FORTY-FOUR

At the end of July 2006, Fidel Castro fell ill, and like the rest of Cuba and the world, we heard the rumors and wondered what they would mean for us.

Even Venezuelan President Hugo Chavez, a strong ally of Cuba, suggested the 79-year-old leader was close to death. "He's fighting a great battle," he said on television in early August.

The news excited our spirits. We didn't miss one BBC or Radio Martí broadcast. We looked for information from everyone's embassies by phone or asked family members for information. In Miami, some exiles fixed up boats so they could sail to Cuba, people waved Cuban flags in the streets, the city council designated the Orange Bowl as a gathering site for revelers, and

Miami-Dade opened its emergency operations center in case celebrations got out of control.

The big question on everyone's mind: Was Fidel Castro dead?

Patel, a fellow inmate, was an Indian who'd been living in Cuba, and he made daily, comic inquiries about Castro's health. Patel had been arrested for helping people escape the country, but since his Cuban wife had a high-ranking brother in the military, he got special consideration. And it didn't hurt that he would rat out anybody for anything. He wasn't a nice guy, but he was funny.

"Confirm?" Patel would ask each day. "Unconfirm?"

The prisoners were as curious as the jailers. Knowing that Fidel Castro was the one man who put us in this prison, as well as the one man who kept us here, all of us, even the religious prisoners, prayed for his death. We had heard that he had a digestive system ailment so severe that Cuban doctors did not have the expertise to help him.

Fidel relinquished power temporarily to Raul Castro, the dictator's little brother, the defense minister and the No. 2 man. Amazing things started happening. Prison officials walked around with worried looks on their faces. Almost all of the propaganda on the television against the United States disappeared, as well as the endless TV homages to the 1959 revolution. It seemed there would be no turning back to the tired old communist rhetoric that kept the Cuban people brain-washed. We continued to hear rumors of Fidel's death and waited for confirmation. Surely he would die. It was just a matter of time.

By September, a photo of the weakened leader appeared in an official newspaper with a note claiming the worst was behind him. In October, clips of him walking and talking on the phone appeared on TV. In December he failed to appear for a meeting of the National Assembly, and we remained hopeful that his era was ending.

We all felt no doctor would be interested in saving the life of the world's longest-serving dictators. We were wrong. A surgeon from Spain loaded all the equipment he needed on a jet, flew to Havana and examined Fidel Castro. Dr. José Luis García Sabrido told reporters in December that Castro was stable and recovering.

In February, Venezuelan President Hugo Chavez interviewed Castro on his nightly radio show. Castro said he was "very well," in English, sending a distinct message to his neighbor to the north.

Our worst fears were confirmed. He was recovering. In 2008, Raul would be elected officially as president, but Fidel would still cast a shadow over his country and his government.

All the old propaganda and communist crap reappeared on the TV.

"Cry, cry, cry!" we said.

And Monir repeated our customary refrain: "Take it like a man!"

CHAPTER FORTY-FIVE

Then started a string of very dark years. I had been in prison for four years and had another nine and a half to go before I completed half my sentence. Fidel Castro was keeping almost all his foreign prisoners for half their sentences, and the few that got out before half were very lucky indeed. Since I was an American, it was possible I would have to serve the whole twenty-five years. No one knew. Not the prison officials, not the people from the Ministry of Justice nor the consul at the U.S. Interests Section. Only the wizard, Fidel Castro, could decide my release date. I was resigned to the fact I was waiting for Fidel Castro to die.

I quietly began gathering pills from other prisoners, tranquilizers I called blue mountains. One night, I took all the blue mountains, painfully chasing them down with water. It was hard. My subconscious fought me. I choked them down and lay on my bed, waiting for them to knock me out. It took four hours to find sleep. I worried about shaming my family. I imagined Carmen getting the news. I wondered if my death would create publicity that would help my fellow inmates. Finally, I drifted off, never expecting to wake up. I awoke to another prisoner shaking me, my scheduled opponent in a tennis match that morning. I told him I was sick and, after I was counted, went back to bed, groggy but very much alive.

After that, I collected little sedatives I called white stars until I had fifty of them. Enough of them, I knew, could stop my heart. I cut the finger off a latex glove, put the pills inside and kept them in a hidden nook of my shaving kit. It gave me comfort to know they were there, but I didn't know if I would again have the courage to go through the ordeal of taking them.

One day, prison officials came to give us a speech and told us they were going to try an experiment. Because the embassies had been complaining of the 110-degree heat in the buildings, they were going to give us one and a half hours of time in the prison yard right after dinner. This was early spring, and there was still plenty of daylight for exercise and other activities outside. Five of us, Maurice, Nazir, Edgar, Monir and myself, would take our plastic chairs, put them in a corner, and spend our hour and a half in conversation. I was fast approaching fifty years old, and the other men were much older, with Maurice being the oldest. I nicknamed our discussion group the Cemetery Club. It was meant as gallows humor, but we reveled in that on a daily basis. I believed that I was too old to survive here, therefore the other guys were sure to die here before me.

"We need to claim our burial plots in the other corner of the prison yard," Edgar joked.

"Yes," I said, "right along the fence that borders the road. That way, after midnight, we can come up out of the ground on the other side of the fence and go, bones clanking, down the road to town and have a few beers."

I was sitting with Monir in the Cemetery Club one evening when he told me a story that illustrates the fear every Cuban lives under. In the Combinado "special area," where the foreigners were imprisoned, there was a man who was nicknamed Big Dimitri. He was a Russian mobster who had crossed Fidel. He was arrogant and unlikable, as you might expect. Little Dimitri, who was Rudy and Peter's traveling partner, was also Russian, and they hated each other. Little Dimitri had paid a Cuban on the outside to make prank phone calls to Big Dimitri. The Cuban would cuss him out and tell him what a piece of crap he was, until one day the re-educator was walking by the telephone when Big Dimitri was receiving one of these calls. Big Dimitri briefly explain to the re-educator what was happening, and the re-educator grabbed the telephone and shouted

at the Cuban, saying who he was and his rank in the
Cuban Ministry of the interior. The re-educator
demanded to know what the Cuban's name was and
why he was making the calls. The Cuban was too afraid
to hang up the phone and proceeded to give the re-
educator his full name, address and national identity
number. He cried to the re-educator that Little Dimitri
had been paying him to make the phone calls and he
needed money to feed his family. All he'd had to do was
hang up the phone, but instead he ratted out himself
and Little Dimitri. The Cubans live in such pervasive
fear that ninety-five percent of Cubans would have done
the same thing. The re-educator admonished the caller
not to do such a thing ever again but did not send the
police after him. Little Dimitri went to solitary
confinement.

From time to time, Perry or other prisoners would
join us in conversation. In good gallows humor, people
would stop by to pay their respects and chat for a while
with us old guys. But after Maurice died, most men
didn't think it was a good idea to have anything to do
with the Cemetery Club. And without Edgar, it was
always just Nazir, Monir and myself. We got no visitors
within ten feet of us.

CHAPTER FORTY-SIX

In the spring of 2007, Edgar started having severe lower back pain. With no diagnostic facilities at the prison infirmary, Edgar needed to see a specialist. But there was an evil Cuban woman who did the scheduling for such trips. She told Edgar she had lived with back pain all her life and that he should get used to it. Soon his bowels and bladder were not working properly, and he was feeling numbness in his legs. The numbness caused him to collapse one evening as a prison official watched. Finally, he was going to get a trip to the prison hospital at Combinado to see a specialist. We would get reports back from other prisoners that they were doing nothing for Edgar, just letting him lie in a hospital bed in pain without control of his bodily functions.

About this time, I read a *Herald Tribune* article that

discussed a study of back pain and whether surgery should be performed on a slipped disc. One paragraph in the article stated that surgery always needed to be performed if the patient showed signs of a pinched nerve in the spinal cord, such as loss of bodily functions and numbness in the legs. Left untreated, the pinched nerve would eventually shut down body organs. I relayed this information to one of the Netherlands prisoners, and they called their embassy to convey it. The symptoms were almost exactly what Edgar had. The Netherlands Embassy had meetings with the hospital doctors and a prisoner welfare official flew from The Netherlands to discuss the issue with the doctors, all to no avail. We continued to hear reports of Edgar lying on a stretcher on the floor of the prison hospital, all day long, in his own filth. Cuban prisoners who worked as orderlies in the hospital had called the treatment of Edgar criminal. Someone had decided that Edgar had lived too much. Only Fidel Castro could give that order. In June 2007, Edgar died, and his Cuban autopsy said it was death by natural causes. If the family wanted his body back so they could perform their own autopsy, it would cost fifteen thousand dollars plus air freight. At sixty years old, Edgar went from bad back pain to death in four months and was buried in an unmarked grave somewhere in Fidel land.

CHAPTER FORTY-SEVEN

With no positive energy in my spirit, I seemed to be overtaken by health problems. Cuban prison is not the place to receive modern medicine. The doctors that were available to us were twenty-one- and twenty-two-year-old interns from a medical school system that was similar to four-year vocational training. They were still practicing medicine with 1959 techniques. There were compassionate and caring nurses at La Condesa, and I might not have survived without them. I got to know some of them well, and from them, I learned how hard daily Cuban life is. I would give them ten or twenty dollars from time to time, and since it was equal to about one month's wages, they were able to get things they badly needed.

Becoming institutionalized has its advantages. I

didn't care about anything. I would start my day and do exactly the same thing I did the previous one. I was still getting my newspapers, magazines and the great books from Perry's sister Corey. By reading eight or more hours a day, both current events as well as fiction, I was able to pass the time without any drama. The rats had multiplied outside to the hundreds, we would go most days with long electrical blackouts, or the water pump would go out on the well and we would have to carry our water in buckets from a tank on a cart pulled by two oxen. The roof would leak everywhere, the food or the water would make people sick daily, but none of it mattered. As long as I had something to read, I could survive.

I also took notes in microscopic handwriting in a minuscule Day-Timer that also had money hidden under its lining. I always kept it with me. Sometimes I inscribed records of what happened. Sometimes I wrote my thoughts. And sometimes I jotted down quotes and phrases in articles I'd read and went over them in my mind. Here in Cuba, we were "innocent until proven powerless." Sometimes, I couldn't help having an "attack of hope," because it was hard not having a soul. I marveled at a Cuban official saying, "The Americans will find out we do not have horns or eat children," when the Cubans had put dissidents and some foreigners in jail for no reason and, in my eyes, had bigger horns than anyone else on the planet. I found the saying "We have respect for the police; we know that they stand between us and the barbarians" wholly ironic, because in Cuba, the police *were* the barbarians. I had no faith in what they called the justice system, with its flawless conviction rate; "an unjust procedure," I wrote, "would undoubtedly lead to unjust results."

CHAPTER FORTY-EIGHT

The spring of 2008 was the primary season for the American presidential elections. We listened to the BBC daily, but I was also able to find an AM broadcast I picked up out of Marathon, Florida. Five or six men would gather around, but not too close, as the Cemetery Club sat and listened to the Bill O'Reilly show to catch the latest poll numbers and O'Reilly's commentary and guests. Everyone was certain that a Democrat would win the general election.

Nazir was an Oxford-educated man from Pakistan but still believed in the Pakistan-style politics of political dynasties. He liked the idea of having a Bush, then a Clinton, another Bush and one more Clinton. Most of the other prisoners wanted Obama to win, either because he was a man of color as they were or because he was the best chance to be nice to Fidel Castro so we could get the hell out of here, as I believed. Every day as we listened, Nazir was chanting, "Hillary! Hillary! Hillary!" And I was chanting, "Barack Obama! Barack Obama! Take me home to my mama!"

Perry, being from the conservative bastion of Alberta, Canada, wanted John McCain to be president. If he had to stay here another four years, so be it.

CHAPTER FORTY-NINE

In May 2008, a prisoner named Eronio, from the island of Curaçao, but living in The Netherlands before his imprisonment, showed me a photograph of a Cuban woman, asking if I would be interested in having a visit from her. She was the friend of Eronio's Cuban woman. All the other prisoners at La Condesa could get a Cuban woman for visits and to do their shopping for them. But not Americans. We didn't even try. The whole process to get a Cuban girlfriend took a fair amount of kissing the asses of the re-educators and other prison officials, something that I wasn't willing to do. The photograph showed the woman pouring a pitcher of milk over her naked body. The liquid's flow maximized her modesty. This was the artistic work of a photographer with multiple exposures in a dark room, but I thought she must have a good attitude to pose for the photograph, and I told Eronio to have her write me a letter.

When the letter arrived and I got it translated, I found her to be a charming and unusual young Cuban woman. After a few letters and phone calls back and forth, I learned she was only twenty-three years old. She looked more like thirty-three years old in the photograph. I had never been attracted to younger women, but I was intrigued by this girl. She hadn't had any children, and she had never been married, unusual in Cuban women. We continued writing letters, and I found her mature for her age, with a great sense of humor. I felt ashamed about the age difference but thought, what the hell, my family won't know, so I have no one to embarrass.

I went to the re-educator and requested a visit from the Cuban woman. He looked at me and, trying not to laugh, asked for her name, address and ID number. Every Cuban under Fidel Castro's dictatorship was issued a number that told any official when they were born and where their home was. In Cuba, your home is where you were born, and that's where you will stay. Cubans are not allowed to move to another city of their choice. The re-educators said that he would have her checked out by state security and I would learn later if the visit was approved. Now I was the one trying not to laugh, because I knew they would not give me a visit since I was an American. I was the enemy.

CHAPTER FIFTY

She had kind of a crazy Cuban first name that I didn't care for, but in one of her letters, she mentioned that her family nickname was Kiki. Kiki fit her well. Kiki Santana was her name. I had sent her some money previously through Eronio's girlfriend, but he mentioned one day that I could write an authorization for her to pick up money personally at the finance window, which was located just outside the prison fence. I would then be able to get a look at her through the cracks in the fence.

The process of the finance window handing out prisoners' money to their Cuban girlfriends is lengthy. The Cubans love their paperwork. I was peering through the different cracks in the fence from a distance of ten yards as each woman would approach the window to receive her money. Some of the other prisoners were laughing at me, knowing that my potential Cuban girlfriend was coming today for the first time. A woman with blond hair came up to the window, but her back was toward me, so I said, "Hola!" She turned around, and her face looked kind of like Kiki's from the photograph I had, but she appeared to be a woman in her mid-forties. She didn't seem to recognize my voice and turned around to face the finance window. I decided that it could not be Kiki. This woman was too old. Five or six more women came to the finance window. None of them were Kiki. I was going to give up.

"No, wait," said Eronio. "She's out there."

Finally, I saw a blonde approaching the finance window dressed in a red and white outfit, and I shouted, "Kiki!" She turned to look at the fence, smile and wave, and my whole body began to shake. Kiki was one of the most beautiful young women I have ever seen in my life, ten times more attractive than her photograph. She had a wonderfully warm smile beaming right at me. I felt, this can't be; I can't be this lucky. But there she was to collect some of my money, which would help ease the hardship of Cuban life for her and her family.

Eronio came over and got a glimpse of her. "Oh, my God," he said. Eronio had done some pimp work in the Netherlands, so it had been natural for him to ask for a fee when he had showed me her photograph three months earlier. The agreed-upon fee had been a hundred and fifty dollars, and now Eronio felt it should be renegotiated to a thousand dollars. But the fee wasn't due until her visit was approved by the prison officials. I rethought my situation. I wasn't lucky, because there was no way the prison officials would allow me such a beautiful young Cuban girlfriend. I would never experience her companionship and affection. This would just be more psychological torture on top of the seven and a half years previously administered to me.

My three-years-long depression lifted instantly. I felt like going to battle. As I walked directly toward the re-educator's office, I couldn't recall the last time that my legs moved so freely and effortlessly. I got in line behind the other prisoners that were there to beg for one thing or another. I had learned that the first step would be an interview of Kiki by the re-educators.

Mighty Mouse was on duty that day. I asked him to schedule an interview with Kiki, and after ten minutes of him trying to discourage me from having a Cuban girlfriend altogether, he finally relented and asked me what day she was available. I knew Mighty Mouse's day off, and that's the day I said she was available. The Cuban soldier that served as the re-educator on that day was young, reasonable and had no desire to repress Americans. Mighty Mouse wrote it in his book, not realizing that I was putting something past him.

The day Kiki came for her interview passed uneventfully. The young re-educator asked just the questions that were required and explained to Kiki that she had to pass the state security background check and get a medical examination as well. She understood this would be the case and said there would be no problem with either. Mercedes, my favorite nurse, had seen her and knew who she was but didn't make any comments to the prison officials, nor did the young re-educator say anything. Consequently the state security background check went quickly, and Kiki got her medical papers. The problem started when Kiki brought the medical papers to La Condesa and the prison officials saw her and realized this young beautiful woman could not be allowed to have visits with one of the Americans, the enemy.

I spent the next five months ranting and raving about extrajudicial repression of the American prisoners, me specifically, to every prison official who came within earshot. I also wrote letters to the Ministry of Justice and the United Nations and blasted the consuls when they visited about the injustice of my visit with Kiki not being approved. Actually, it had not been denied; the officials just said I had to wait. All the other foreign prisoners' visits had been approved within two months, and I knew they were just trying to wear me down and make me give up. But I kept battling, if for no other reason than the battle made me feel alive.

In December 2008, Daniel, who had been a re-educator for many years but was now one of the head prison officials, approached me with a smile on his face and told me my visit had been approved. I actually couldn't help myself and gave him a bear hug. He was obviously embarrassed but congratulated me and said to see the re-educator for a visit schedule. Kiki and I would have a three-hour visit in the visiting rooms, then, three weeks later, a three-hour visit known as pavilion, the conjugal visits. This schedule would continue, with rotating visits every three weeks. I was going to spend three hours in a bed with a Cuban goddess twenty-six years younger than I. Suddenly I felt I wasn't in hell any longer. I would need to get some of that copycat Viagra being sold in the prison, as well as get this forty-nine-year-old body on a strenuous exercise routine to prepare myself for the glorious day to come.

After wearing the same shirts for years, I also worked on buying newer clothes from other prisoners who'd received extras from their loved ones. I couldn't get new sneakers, but after one bad experience buying plastic Chinese shoes that fell apart, I bought used sneakers from my fellow prisoners. There were cobblers in prison who would stitch and re-stitch inmates' shoes with thread they'd extracted from burlap sacks. With bits of leather or replacement soles sewn in over time, these Frankenshoes were better than new plastic shoes that wore out in three months.

CHAPTER FIFTY-ONE

Barack Obama had been elected president the previous month, and the whole world seemed happy to have the George W. Bush years relegated to history — I believed none more so than Fidel Castro. I had never believed that my jailers would allow me a visit with a Cuban girlfriend, and if left up to the prison officials, I would not have. But in Cuba, all actions come from the top, and the prison officials were told to let up on the repression of the Americans. Not only were my visits approved, but the officials' daily repressive actions seemed to stop. Thank you, Barack Obama! I was on the hope-and-change bandwagon. After six years in the Hotel Fidel Castro, my next hope was, Barack Obama, Barack Obama, take me home to my mama!

Kiki had assured me in earlier discussions that it was common and generally accepted for middle-aged men to have young women as girlfriends and even wives in Cuba. I knew that in the United States, only rich men were so lucky. I could not help but think these young Cuban women could not stand the thought of living in the same three-room house where they were born — living with their parents, brothers and sisters, and their spouses and new children, indefinitely. Middle-aged men had their own house. It was a form of escape. Kiki's desire was to escape to the United States. I was to be her ticket out. Who was I to say no?

The day of her first visit, I waited with apprehension for her to come through the gate in the prison fence. The visit rooms were in a part of the prison adjacent to the exercise yard. There were a hundred men in the yard that day, and I was not waiting alone. Most of them were close to the gate so they could get a look at Kiki. When she came through, it reminded me of a princess stepping out to greet the commoners. Most of the men just stood and gawked, but a few bold ones called greetings to her, which she returned in a warm and gracious manner. I still couldn't believe she was here to see me.

One of the men who cooks had made us a pizza in a skillet on a Cuban hot plate. I had a bottle of Cuban cola, along with ice from my refrigerator and a package of cookies for dessert. Kiki was impressed. We laughed, shared some new stories, referred to my Spanish-English dictionary frequently and connected even better than we had through six months of letter-writing.

CHAPTER FIFTY-TWO

Even after six years at the Hotel Fidel Castro, my Spanish was still very bad. Our letters to each other were usually five or six pages. I never attempted to write in Spanish. Nicanor did that. Nicanor had the bunk below me and was always available to translate at the rate of one pack of cigarettes per page. He was from Belize and had mixed Spanish and Mayan Indian heritage. He was a small guy with a funny-looking face. He was very intelligent and had a hilarious sense of humor, but if he wasn't making me laugh with what he had said, I was always laughing inside as I looked at that funny face. He was always making something. He carved model ships from blocks of wood, model helicopters out of plastic roll-on deodorant bottles and many other imaginative items. He had been studying architecture at a university in Cuba when he was accused of somehow helping people escape from the country. There was never any evidence or testimony that he'd committed a crime, but Fidel must have wanted a Belize prisoner. Fidel Castro had said on television that his prisons were like universities, so I guess you could call it a transfer. Nicanor had served three years of a seven-year sentence.

Because Nicanor translated all of our letters, he got to know Kiki very well. They were about the same age and same height, and when he met her in person, I could tell he wanted his own Kiki just like that one. I adored her and came to love her very much, but Nicanor was head over heels in love at the sight of that beautiful young woman. He wanted to know if she had a sister. All the prisoners wanted to know if she had a sister. Through all my years in Cuban prison, more than a hundred women must have come through the gate for visits, but none more lovely than Kiki.

I had always had a very structured routine for my daily prison life, so much so that Nicanor and Monir would call me the robot. I went about my routine and looked toward the future in three-week intervals leading up to my visits with Kiki. I continued to spend three hundred dollars a year on old newspapers and maga-zines, reading every word on every page. Perry's sister Corey was still bringing thirty new books every three months. BBC on the shortwave radio and discussions of politics and current events with Monir and Nazir continued daily. But the approaching visits with Kiki were always foremost in my mind.

By 2009, hope and change had not trickled down to Cuba and Hotel Fidel Castro. But by then I was fully institutionalized. My first six years were pure hell, but with Kiki in my life, I could do another six years. Twelve years would be one half of my sentence. Kiki didn't like the sound of that and believed I would be released sooner. No one ever had any idea when they were going to be released. I had watched a hundred prisoners go over the years, but Fidel Castro never gave anyone a release date they could look forward to. Just part of the Stalinist psychological torture.

CHAPTER FIFTY-THREE

A Frenchman named Jean Louis had been living in Cuba for a number of years. He had become involved in purchasing boats from the Cuban government that they had seized for one reason or another. If a government official or state security man didn't like someone, and that someone owned a boat, the official would seize it and fabricate a reason for doing so. International maritime law did not apply in Fidel's Cuba. Jean Louis would purchase these boats at a fraction of their worth, clean them up and repair them, and take them out of Cuba to be sold. It had been a quite a lucrative business for him until one of the boats he sold was found in Europe, loaded with dope from South America. The buyers had not transferred the boat into their name, and INTERPOL had come calling to the Cuban national police. Jean Louis explained to them that he just fixed up the boats and sold them. But Cuba had been embarrassed by the incident, and someone had to pay with a prison sentence.

When Jean Louis came to La Condesa, he was sure it was all a big mistake that would be corrected. Just like many men who came before him, he was certain his stay at La Condesa was only temporary. He was confident because, he would say in his French accent, he knew these people, he worked with these people, he lived with these people for many years. "These are good people!" he would proclaim. Needless to say, Monir and I, and everyone else for that matter, would laugh at his proclamation. He would spend one year waiting for his court date, and Monir and I spent one year wondering whether he would take it like a man or cry, cry, cry. He received a fifteen-year sentence but remained in complete denial that this injustice had happened to him, stating that the sentence meant nothing. He and the French government were working on something else that would get him freed shortly.

It dawned on Monir and I that a prisoner has to accept reality before he can make the decision to take it like a man, or cry, cry, cry. If a man stays delusional, he might be able to avoid despair and hopelessness. We contemplated the idea and decided the path of delusion had merit. It was too late for us, but we could tell all the new prisoners, don't worry, you all will be going home very soon. We both laughed, but Monir proceeded to do just that with many of the new prisoners that walked through the gate. Monir's sense of humor was that of a straight man comedian, so he could pull it off easily. His message was too cruel for me to pull off, but I watched these new prisoners when Monir told them that, and their faces would light up with joy. He would justify it by saying, now they have three choices, cry, cry, cry; take it like a man; or remain in delusional denial.

CHAPTER FIFTY-FOUR

Through 2009, the Cuban prison officials had been slowly renovating a building outside of the south fence at La Condesa. It had been the minimum security housing for prisoners at the end of their sentences. It was unused for five years while Fidel worked his wizardry to crush our spirit and keep us occupied with despair. But now, we had a kinder, gentler Castro. I was denied the minimum severity classification, even though I had reached the allotted time in my sentence. When the renovation was finished, the jailers moved sixty-five long-term prisoners over to the minimum security side. Perry, Monir, Nazir, and almost all the other men I had daily conversations with were now there. I would have to stay in building two for nine more months. Nicanor had been released. They had snuck Capt. Know-It-All into building two while I was away at the Combinado prison hospital, receiving some Cuban doctor butchery; by that, I mean surgery for an infection that the nurses had no antibiotics to treat. I got the U.S. Interests Section to supply gloves for when they treated me, because they had no soap to wash their hands.

When I came back to La Condesa, Capt. Know-It-All told me he felt the Cubans were trying to kill him because they left him in building one for so long. I liked the sound of that. Having to look at his face several times daily now did not make me happy. Other prisoners mocked his absurd, bombastic speeches as he used big words the non-English speakers would never know. Kevin was good at convincing people he knew more than he did. He was the kind of guy who never laughed at himself, who did his best to cover up his inclinations toward bad judgment. People like him are dangerous, because they can take others in — and take them down with him. Everyone at La Condesa called him Capt. Know-It-All when they learned his story.

In August 2010, Kiki turned up pregnant. I had gotten a vasectomy eleven years earlier, so we both knew the baby was not mine. I had never questioned her about other relationships. She was a beautiful young woman, and I never expected her to be monogamous. Her Cuban doctor had told her in the past that with her reproductive health problems, she would have trouble getting pregnant. I had explained back then that American doctors had numerous techniques of modern medicine to achieve that goal against all obstacles. But the Cuban doctor told her again that she should continue with the pregnancy, because it might be her only chance. Kiki asked me what she should do, but I did not feel comfortable telling her she should have an abortion and wait till she got to the United States to start a family. I wanted her to make the decision for herself. She chose to be a mother. I would never see Kiki again, and prison life at the Hotel Fidel Castro once again became hell.

CHAPTER FIFTY-FIVE

There had been an American of Cuban parents who had been at La Condesa for three and a half years. His name was Hector, and he got his sentence because he was in a traffic accident that had killed a Cuban. It wasn't drunk driving or a serious infraction on his part, but in Cuba, if someone dies in a car accident, someone goes to prison. Hector had been out about one year and maintained close contact with Rudy the Russian and a Bahamian named Judd. Hector was a generous young man and sent through Rudy's girlfriend two Sirius pocket satellite radios. I overheard a conversation of theirs and immediately knew what they had. I had tried to get an XM radio into the prison two years previously through legitimate channels, but the officials said no. A hundred thirty-five channels to choose from was a hundred thirty-three too many for the Hotel Fidel Castro.

My family had blown three hundred dollars on that wasted effort, because they never got the radio back. But I offered four hundred twenty-five dollars for either one of them. Rudy said no, but Judd said yes. Hallelujah! We got them turned on through Rudy's mother in Chicago, and we both had a hundred thirty-five channels to tune out the despair-generating cacophony of our daily prison life. Not only could I listen to my favorite old rock music; it had all the major news organizations' audio, as well as American sports channels. An information junkie, I was now able to get news in real time, not just from my two-month-old newspapers and magazines or bad BBC shortwave. It looked like a very small, inexpensive MP3 player, and the antenna was built into the headphones. These were super contraband, but none of the officials ever looked twice at it. I would finish out my Cuban prison time always protecting this radio and being eternally grateful to Hector, Judd, Rudy and his girlfriend, who smuggled it in.

Edgar was no longer with us, having died in 2007, so I didn't have him to share Ronnie James Dio lyrics with, but I was able to record twenty or more Dio songs from the rock channels on my Sirius radio, and very soon they were playing in my head almost constantly whether I had the radio on or not. It seemed almost every song's lyrics had a parallel in this existence of mind-numbing despair. In the spring of 2010, I was listening to one of the rock channels when they announced a special to commemorate the passing of Ronnie James Dio. I had heard nothing about him having stomach cancer. I had met him back in the mid-1980s and was amazed that his powerful voice could come from such a small man. Here in Cuba, his lyrics wove through this deprivation of sight, sound and thought that was always with me.

CHAPTER FIFTY-SIX

In the fall of 2010, I was finally classified as minimum severity. But there were no bunks available over in the minimum-security building, because Fidel was not releasing any hostages. So I had to wait until the spring of 2011 before I was finally moved out of building two and away from Capt. Know-It-All once again. I hid my satellite radio in my suitcase, which was in a deep storage room. I knew that I and my things would be thoroughly searched before switching to minimum security, outside of the prison fence. The prisoners in minimum were allowed to come back inside the prison to buy things at the shop or retrieve deep storage items, as well as use the exercise yard, one hour each day. I would return the following day to retrieve my satellite radio.

The minimum security building had the main

prison fence on its north side but just a decorative iron
fence facing south and west. There were also shade trees
under which we could sit in our plastic chairs. Here we
were able to view the road and its travelers and watch
the sugarcane growing around the Hotel Fidel Castro.
After eight years of not being able to see outside the
prison walls and neither breeze nor shade, this was
damn near civilized. There was only one guard who
would sit and observe us, never telling us what we could
or could not do. Monir, Nazir, Roderigo and sometimes
Perry would sit outside and discuss the news that I was
getting through my satellite radio. Rasta was here, as
well as most of the men arrested in 2002 or 2003. Even
the ones that I found intolerable for years began acting
like gentlemen in these new surroundings. Feng shui? It
was as good as it gets in Cuba.

When they had renovated this building the previous
year, the officials had put in a small stove, oven, one
freezer and one refrigerator. All the prisoners who had
owned stoves and, more important, refrigerators, had to
leave them behind. Consequently, the vegetables would
deteriorate quickly, because there was not room for
them in the one refrigerator. After enough complaining
of not having fresh vegetables, some prisoners were
allowed to start a garden just to the south of the minimum-security building fence. It started with three prisoners, but soon twenty prisoners had their own patch of
ground. It was a welcome diversion for these men to be

able to tend to their vegetable plants. The prison
kitchen got its share of the harvest, and the prison officials took what they wanted, when they wanted. After
nine years, it was wonderful to taste fresh vegetables
again, not the two-week-old ones we were used to.

CHAPTER FIFTY-SEVEN

There was a Canadian here in minimum security who had been living in a small town in southwest Cuba. For five years, he had helped the community with everything from roof repair to water projects and felt really close to the Cubans there. He never exploited them, just enjoyed the simple life that the place offered. He was able to do so without much discomfort, because he had the money to build his own house and furnish it with what he needed from Canada. The community was very appreciative for all his efforts to help them, but the Cuban state security was not. The proper belief is that Fidel's revolution takes care of everyone's needs, and this man was disruptive to that dogma. So officials fabricated a case against him; instilled the proper fear in the community, which then turned against him; and put him in prison with a relatively mild seven-year sentence.

One early morning, another long-term prisoner and I were making coffee when the Canadian appeared in a tank top, displaying an unusual tattoo on his upper arm. The tattoo displayed a waving Canadian flag blending with a waving Cuban flag. It was quite artistic and in full color. Above the tattoo were the words "Canadian Cuban friendship," with the Spanish translation below it. The other prisoner and myself looked at the tattoo and, knowing his story, started laughing. When we stopped, we looked at each other and simultaneously said, "How do you like me now?" We laughed again for so long, our coffee got cold.

In the summer of 2011, some of the men who had been playing golf on their Sony handheld devices decided that they liked the game. In the early years, the brooms that were available to sweep the prison floor were handmade out of straw, tied with string to a straight branch. They were so ineffective that some of the men had their girlfriends buy plastic brooms. They had a straight wood handle that screwed into a plastic T that held the bristles. These brooms would be used until the bristles had worn down to a half an inch. One of the golf video gamers cut the plastic T in half, making it L-shaped, removed the remaining bristles, and shortened the handle to three feet. He now had what crudely resembled a putter. He found an old tennis ball and proceeded to excavate eighteen holes the size of that tennis ball in the minimum security prison yard. He named each hole after one of the famous golf courses that were on his Sony PSP. After assigning a par value to each hole, there was an eighteen-hole golf course in the prison yard of La Condesa minimum security. Within two weeks, ten men had made themselves golf clubs and were playing at least eighteen holes daily. Maybe one or two had actually held a golf club in their hand, but all were trying to be competitive and would improve with each day. Since my daily routine never varied, it wasn't until October 2011 that I finally gave in and made myself a putter as well as a chipper out of new brooms from the prison shop. By then, five of the other men were very good at this prison golf game, and for me, trying but failing to direct a bouncing tennis ball over rocks in the ground and around tree roots never allowed me to be among the top players.

In November 2011, Perry was told he would be freed in the next couple of days. He couldn't be sure if it was true or not, because they had told him many years ago that he would be freed only to be told the week later it was a mistake. Perry gave away his prison stuff. With his family coming to visit every four months, he had accumulated eight suitcases of unconsumed free-world crap in the deep storage room. Four days later he was gone, after more than nine years in Cuban prison for nothing other than Fidel Castro's decision to take hostages in his diplomatic war with the free world. Four other long-term prisoners were also released that month, so it appeared that things were starting to move in the right direction.

CHAPTER FIFTY-EIGHT

When Perry departed, he left me cans of tuna fish. His gift became more important than he could have realized, not just to me, but to a friend I was about to make.

A sewer line ran out of the bathrooms and along the back of the visitors' building, and like everything else here, it was in poor condition. One day, one of the prisoners accustomed to feeding cats in back of the building heard soft cries from a crack in the pipe. He opened the hole a little wider and pulled out the source of the noise: a scrawny, injured, half-dead kitten.

He was so thin, I could see his bones. His eyes were bugging out. Half his fur was gone, probably from fighting rats, though our rat population had diminished since the prison started allowing us to take care of several stray cats that would hang out in the yard.

I thought it had a will to live and started feeding it Perry's precious tuna fish. But a fellow inmate, trying to be helpful, gave it an antibiotic that nearly killed it.

For five days, the kitten was almost comatose. I wrapped him up and nursed him, feeding him a little every day until he got better. We developed a bond that became apparent when I took him out during my daily exercise. I'd go to the far end of the yard and call him. He would try to follow, but, still weak, the kitten would often fall down, get up, look around in fear of pursuing rats, and follow me again. Every day, he got a little better, and by January, he had his fur back and would play with me, swatting at pieces of string. He still followed me as I did my shoulder presses and laps around the yard, and my fellow prisoners had a good laugh at the gringo with the devoted cat. The guards weren't impressed, because the cat was eating better than they were, and he slept snug in a box I'd made up for him with a towel for bedding.

I called him Tigre. He was one of those cats seen frequently in Cuba who are gray-brown with distinctive black tiger stripes that wrapped around a white belly.

I had one of the best plastic chairs in the place. I'd traded pots and pans for it, knowing I wouldn't cook. The chair had a nice, high back, and I had cushions made for it with covers I could swap out and wash. My seat became Tigre's seat. If I wasn't in it, the cat would jump right up and take my place. I kept the chair in front of my bunk near the door, and Tigre made it his home.

When it was raining, all the cats liked to sleep inside, and Tigre learned to jump up and through the window to get into my cell. I would wake up and find him sleeping in the chair. I'd always liked dogs and was never a cat person, but Tigre became a good friend.

CHAPTER FIFTY-NINE

One evening the following month, prison Capt. Sermiento strolled in with two other officials. They didn't say anything but proceeded to sit in a couple of the plastic chairs in front of the television. It kind of spooked us, but when we saw Raul Castro appear on the television, the volume went up, and everyone gathered around. He started his speech with the typical communist crap about the glory of the revolution of 1959. Some prisoners wandered off, but others felt he was going to say something important, so they pulled up a chair. And he did.

He announced that Cuba was going to release more than three thousand prisoners, including eighty-six foreigners, in the coming months. It would be a full amnesty, with all crimes against Cuba and the revolution forgiven. Someone asked Sermiento what that meant, and he responded with, "Most all of you will be gone soon." I could tell from Sermiento's face that he wasn't happy. Although he loved the new prisoners with their look of disbelief and bewilderment, we were his long-term prisoners, and he took joy in seeing our cumulative despair. He and the other officials were not there to share our joy in this moment. They were there to maintain order in case our exuberance overcame their instilled discipline.

Most people didn't believe the announcement, thinking it was just another Cuban tactic in Fidel's battles with the free world. But Roderigo had heard the rumor a week ago. His source was someone inside the Cuban government, and he made plans to telephone his source first thing in the morning to get some details. Sermiento and the other officials left. We gathered in small groups and started contemplating the possibility that it was true. Eighty-six foreigners was more than all of us in this minimum-security building. There were still some men that had been nine years in the main La Condesa prison as well as Combinado prison. Those were the ones with the thirty-year sentences. But if the news were actually true, there was no reason all of us would not be released.

The men who couldn't get on the telephone that night were on the call list first thing in the morning to tell their families the news. The list had thirty or more names on it all day long. Roderigo was able to get through to his Cuban government source, and we got a breakdown of how many prisoners would be released from each country. Three Americans would be set free. Lazaro and I were the only Americans in minimum severity, but there were four others, including Alan Gross, who was serving his sentence at a military hospital. Sharkey was still at Combinado, Capt. Know-It-All in building two, and there was one other American prisoner. All these years, Fidel had always kept five American prisoners to match the five Cuban spies in prison in the United States. He might be abandoning the five for five plan and going with Alan Gross as a lone hostage, considering he was the only one the U.S. government ever showed any interest in having back. But if Lazaro and I were certain to be released, who was the third American? Crap, I thought, it must be Capt. Know-It-All!

The prison golfing tournaments stopped, men abandoned their exercise routines, and the vegetable garden outside the fence went untended. Mighty Mouse had come by and inventoried everyone's possessions, stating that nothing could be left behind for the remaining prisoners. Everything had to be taken out when we left. That was a lot of worthless possessions to haul out. Some men just started throwing things into the garbage, where the other Cuban prisoners could make use of the stuff.

CHAPTER SIXTY

After two weeks when nothing happened, we thought we were seeing another case of Fidel Castro changing his mind. Three weeks, four and five weeks, nothing. After six weeks, the embassies started receiving notification of which of their citizens would be released. It took another week, but finally, Lazaro was told he would be released. I got on the phone and was told that the other two Americans being released were from a prison in Matanzas, Cuba — two people the rest of us didn't even know existed. I was going nowhere. With Lazaro's release, Cuba was back down to five American prisoners. Fidel was sticking with the five for five plan after all. Take it like a man!

Welcome to the Hotel Fidel Castro
such an ugly place, such an ugly face

we're all locked up at the Hotel Fidel Castro
any time of year, you can find us here
our minds are definitely twisted,
but there's no Mercedes Benz
there are lots of furry, furry rats,
but they're not friends
relax in the prison cell, bunk full of sweat
some cry to remember, some cry to forget

I spent the next few days in complete despair. I would sit in my chair with my satellite radio, watching the Cubans go by on the street, while the rest of the men packed their things and exchanged email addresses. Every one of them would come by and talk to me for a few moments to say that I would be released soon. Keep up hope.

The prison officials came, and everyone knew it was with the list of those who would be leaving that first day of deliverance. Forty-six men were very happy, but I wasn't there to share in their happiness, because I had retreated to the back of the building in the showers. I missed the goodbyes that would make me cry, but from a window, I watched them walk out the gate in single file down the road, to the bus that would take them to freedom. I'm sure it was the happiest moment of their lives. In the showers, I could cry alone. Cry. cry, cry. I definitely did not take it like a man.

Most of the other men had been told they were

going but had to wait for travel visas to be arranged, along with plane tickets paid for. Within three weeks, there were only about six of us left out of sixty-four. One of the men who was still there was named Francis. Francis was from the Dominican Republic, a practicing Christian of absurd levels during his prison time, and was writing the Vatican about his being left out of the amnesty. Francis had always been mistrusted because he was too close to the prison officials, and I never hid my disdain for him. But I was touched when he said he included me in the letter, saying that it wasn't fair for Fidel to keep five Americans who had nothing to do with his five spies in American prisons. I thanked him but told him I knew in my heart I would be here until Fidel Castro died.

I wondered if I would ever see my family again. My mother had developed Alzheimer's and its attendant memory loss, so every time she asked my sister how I was doing, my mother went through a new round of shock and anxiety when she heard I was in prison. Her forgetfulness was too painful, and my sister began telling her I was still traveling in the Caribbean. I was on an endless vacation at the Hotel Fidel Castro.

CHAPTER SIXTY-ONE

I spent February and March doing my usual routine, like a robot. Only now I would sit by myself, petting Tigre, watching the sugarcane grow and the deprived Cubans going to and from their fifty-cents-a-day jobs as I listened to the satellite radio. Alan Gross was causing a big stir back home in the states. His story and his plight were on the CNN broadcast with regularity. After nine years and about ten gringo Americans through the Hotel Fidel Castro, he's the only one for whom the U.S. government had cried foul.

One early evening, while surfing through the news channels on my satellite radio, I heard Wolf Blitzer on CNN say the network had a video of a first-ever look inside a Cuban prison. Needless to say, I stopped right there. After the commercial break, he talked about a video taken inside Combinado del Este prison. He spoke about the brave man who'd smuggled it out and identified the person in the video as Douglas Moore. That was Sharkey! Sure enough, I heard the voice of Sharkey describing the filth and deprivation that all prisoners endure at the Hotel Fidel Castro, Big House. This went on for five or six minutes, and I was incredulous that they were able to smuggle the video out of that four-story monument to hell. Castro was going to be pissed. Heads would roll, but they couldn't do anything else to Sharkey that they hadn't already done.

Sharkey had earned his trip from La Condesa to a permanent stay in Combinado by resisting their communist crap daily. They tried to break his will with physical beatings, two-year stretches in solitary confinement and a sentence that had grown from seven years to twenty-five. Sharkey was always a little bent to start with, but by then he had turned into a paranoid and delusional basket case. Still, he was always fearless, the most blindly courageous person I've ever met. He would not only tell the Cuban prison officials what he thought; he was the only one of us Americans who had the courage to tell the U.S. Interests Section consuls of their deficiencies in allowing Castro to keep us as hostages. The rest of us could never have done that, because there was always a chance they might decide to help us. The last time I had spoken to him on the telephone, he was rambling, saying the U.S. government had always been in cahoots with the Castros, a secret conspiracy of fifty years.

I got only the audio of the CNN broadcast, but as I listened to Sharkey's voice, I could picture him giving a tour on camera of the "special area" that had been my squalor for four months many years ago.

After nine years and zero press coverage of the Americans' plight in Cuban prison, in the last month and a half, there had been the Sharkey video and numerous reports about Alan Gross. I hadn't trusted my ability to think straight since I came here, and I couldn't decide if these events were good for me or catastrophic. Fidel might have already given the order for a sunrise firing squad with all American prisoners in attendance. Or maybe, on the other hand, this is what he wanted: American press crying about U.S. citizens in Cuban prisons so he could cry about his five heroes in American prisons.

One day in March, a fellow prisoner came running inside to tell me that Lazaro had just driven by in a car with his Cuban girlfriend. I found that hard to believe, but one of the other men confirmed it. I came to the conclusion that since Fidel Castro gave them all amnesty, he must be able to travel to and from Cuba freely, as if nothing had ever happened. Such travels seemed too risky to me, but Lazaro had family here and was always an easygoing, fearless fellow. The other men thought he would be driving back the other way, so I sat in my plastic chair and waited. The only thing down this old country road was a small community named Rio Seco and the swampy south shore of Cuba, four miles down the road. There was nothing but sugarcane fields in between. Sure enough, an hour later, in a late-model rental car, Lazaro came driving by. He said a few words, smiling and waving while all of us prisoners stood in shocked awe of what it must be like to one day drive a rental car again. I could hardly control my emotions. Monir would have said, "Cry, cry, cry."

CHAPTER SIXTY-TWO

On April 6, 2012, I was doing my regular exercise routine at eight o'clock in the morning. It was a Friday. Mighty Mouse called my name, and I thought, oh, crap, what does he want now? I had spent all my years cringing at the sound of a Cuban prison official calling my name.

"Yes, sir," I answered, while I continued my fast walk from the far side of the building.

"Come here now," he said.

Crap. This usually meant he didn't like the way I made my bunk or some other insignificant observance of his. He had that same blank look on his face as he looked up at mine, a foot above his, as he had done for nine years, the face of a fearless mouse with the full power of Fidel Castro and the revolution behind him.

"You have been given your freedom," he said. "You have one hour to pack your things."

At first I thought it was a joke, but he assured me it wasn't. He also assured me it wasn't a trick to get me in the paddy wagon and take me God knows where, as they had done to Sharkey nine years ago. The few men that were left there were all congratulating me when someone said the Cubans were letting Capt. Know-It-All go as well. If there was one thing I didn't want to hear, that was it. Crap. It was just too much to ask of the heavens for him to stay here and suffer as he should. Another nine years for him would have been fair.

I gave away or threw away everything that I didn't need to get home with. I got rid of the pills I'd been accumulating as a final contingency plan. I hired a couple of guys to carry all my bedding to the far side of the prison and walked out of minimum security with just a small shoulder bag. I had to go to the deep storage room, retrieve my suitcase from there and distribute its contents in the same manner. And there I saw Capt. Know-It-All, who was happy and giggling, and when he looked at me and saw my stony face, he understood. He didn't try to speak to me and would not for the next four days.

I looked at Tigre as I was leaving. The cat was sitting in my chair, which I'd given to someone else. I petted him goodbye. *Take it like a man,* I was telling him. He watched me as I walked out the gate. Everyone loved him as much as I did. I knew he would be all right.

We were put in a minivan that had been dispatched from Cuban immigration detention. What a joke that was. Absolutely no one in their right mind immigrated here, so it was used for foreigners that were crazy, out of money, or prisoners like ourselves, on our way out. They charged sixteen dollars a day and wanted to hear after each meal how great the food was. It was crap. Bonito was the Cuban man who worked at the U.S. Interests Section and, through the years, had handled all of the prisoners' needs by phone. Bonito received our Western Union transfers, sent emails for us and occasionally came to our quarterly consul visits at the prison to translate. He was sent here to immigration detention to take our photograph for new passports as well as collect money for the three-hundred-fifty-dollar, twenty-minute flight to Miami.

We were driven to the airport there in Havana on the following Monday afternoon, April 9. During the immigration detention of three days, Capt. Know-It-All had been in a cell down the hall, not the same one I was in. That was a good thing. When I got to the airport, I checked in with my ticket and confirmed that Bonito was smart enough not to book our seats close to each other. I then changed my Cuban money into American dollars, bee-lined it to the cold drinks kiosk, and bought my first cold beer in nine and a half years. I leisurely drank six of those beers before boarding the plane. That is, about as leisurely as a beer lover could after nine and a half years.

CHAPTER SIXTY-THREE

The plane's wheels left the ground. I gave a Homer Simpson "Woo hoo!" and felt the rush of a thirty-minute high of exhilaration no recreational drug could ever match. After leaving the plane at the Miami airport, I headed straight to the bathroom to get rid of the Cuban beer. The bathroom at that time of night was completely empty, except for Capt. Know-It-All. Through all my years at the hotel Fidel Castro, I had joked with my fellow prisoners that if they let Kevin go the same time as me, I would strangle him on the floor of the Miami international Airport. I had expressed my pledge to well over a hundred men. And here was my opportunity.

Not a chance.

I was a free man now and had every intention of staying that way.

The customs cards that they give you aboard the plane to fill out prior to arrival had a question of whether my travel was business or pleasure. I had left it blank while I contemplated the proper answer. It was still blank when I handed the card to the first customs man I came up to. When he asked me about it, I said nine years of prison was neither business nor, I assured him, pleasure. Naturally, this response got me a trip to the feds' office for an interview.

Behind an unassuming door, what seemed like an entire city of security personnel opened up before me, a teeming, "Get Smart" world of badges and agents. As I was led down the hall, I saw Capt. Know-It-All already seated in one of the small offices. I could only hope that he had an outstanding warrant or something.

The feds wanted to know the story, and I gave them a twenty-minute version. I'm sure I read more than a thousand books while in Cuba, and at least a hundred of those were spy novels or spy nonfiction. So I was hoping for some counterintelligence questions that would decipher whether the Cubans had brainwashed me into becoming a spy for Fidel Castro, or if I had developed nine years of anger toward my own government, wanting to do it harm.

They didn't ask me such things. They were smart young agents and knew that neither could be the case. I felt proud knowing that we had such intelligent young people in the sometimes unintelligent business of law enforcement protecting our country. I was led out of the security section and pointed in the direction of the hotels' courtesy-van telephones. It was a hundred-yard walk, and I was stretching my legs out in a long stride. But I was concerned when I noticed I had five federal agents right on my heels.

"It's eleven o'clock at night," they said, assuaging my fears. "We're all going to the parking garage so we can drive home."

Most men have a bad year sometime in their life. I had just finished a very bad decade in mine. I hoped to God that was the last time I was ever in the presence of five law enforcement officers.

It was like awakening from a bad dream. Here in Miami, with my feet on the ground in America, it felt as if I'd never left. Calling the hotel courtesy phone felt like every other time I'd called one. The shuttle ride was not extraordinary. I didn't feel that bitter or even that different, but I was. I am more blunt now. I'm more like my mother than I ever was; I get emotional when I see a happy movie or hear a sad story. I am finding my purpose in life. I am finding my voice. But I still live on a sailboat. And, unlike so many in Cuba, I am free.

ABOUT THE AUTHOR

Rick Townson lives in Key West, Florida, and spends his time as the captain of Sunshine Charters, exploring the bayside waters of the lower Florida Keys.

sunshinecharterskw.com